AMERICAN INTERVENTION IN THE RUSSIAN CIVIL WAR

Problems in American Civilization

AMERICAN INTERVENTION
in the
RUSSIAN CIVIL WAR

EDITED WITH AN INTRODUCTION BY
Betty Miller Unterberger
TEXAS A. & M. UNIVERSITY

D. C. HEATH AND COMPANY
A division of RAYTHEON EDUCATION COMPANY
LEXINGTON, MASSACHUSETTS

Library of Congress Catalog Card Number: 69-11330

INTRODUCTION

APPROXIMATELY fifty years ago in the late summer of 1918, in the midst of World War I and some nine months after the Bolshevik revolution, an American expeditionary force landed in Russia to participate in a military intervention which was to last until 1920. While contemporary critics of the Wilson administration described the enterprise as "Mr. Wilson's little war with Russia," most Americans today have long since forgotten it. Not so the Russians! Allied intervention has occupied a prominent place in Soviet history and historiography. Soviet leaders as well as historians have repeatedly spoken with bitter reproach of the United States role as hostile promoter and participant in an intervention basically antagonistic to the interests of the Russian people. Indeed, Soviet historic bitterness toward the United States may be traced back not only to American behavior toward the Bolshevik revolution itself but also to American participation in the intervention which followed.

The delicacy and unusual character of the American expedition to Russia was perhaps best revealed by the commander of the force himself, Major General William S. Graves. On August 2, 1918, he had received a secret code message from Washington, directing him to "take the first and fastest train out of San Francisco and proceed to Kansas City." Once there, he was to go to the Baltimore Hotel and ask for the Secretary of War. Graves considered this one of the most remarkable communications that had ever come out of the War Department. He left immediately for Kansas City. There he met Newton D. Baker, Secretary of War, who informed him that he was being sent to Siberia. Baker then handed him a sealed envelope, saying, "This contains the policy of the United States in Russia which you are to follow. Watch your step; you will be walking on eggs loaded with dynamite. God bless you and good-bye." Thus began one of the strangest adventures in American diplomatic and military history.

Regardless of how it affected Soviet attitudes toward the United States, military intervention in Siberia became the most important phase of American foreign policy in the Far East during and immediately following World War I. Its effects were far-reaching, especially as applied to American relations not only with Russia but also with Japan. Intervention initiated a trend in America's policy toward Soviet Russia which was to continue until 1933 and to be applied later in relation to another great Communist power, China. Intervention also introduced America's greatest offensive against Japanese expansion on the Asiatic continent prior to World War II.

In March and November of 1917 Russia had been shaken by two successive revolutions. The first overthrew the Romanov dynasty and established a "liberal" Provisional government. This was hailed with enthusiasm by President Wilson, who had been loath to enter the war with autocratic Russia. However, a democratic Russia was a "fit partner for a League of honor." Thus the United States was the first nation to extend recognition to the new government. The Bolshevik revolution received a far different reception, for its first major act was to demand an immediate general and democratic peace with the Central Powers. Russia ceased military operations and began preliminary peace negotiations.

The Allies and the United States were invited to participate. They did not accept. Neither the peace proposals nor the character of the new Russian government commended themselves to the United States and her Allies. They were naturally suspicious of a revolutionary government which claimed to rule in the name of the proletariat and advocated class war, world revolution and the overthrow of capitalism.

The Soviet decree of February 3, 1918, which repudiated all foreign state loans, scarcely increased Bolshevik popularity with the Allies. To this was added the rumor that the Bolshevik leaders, Lenin and Trotsky, were German agents who had returned to Russia with the assistance of the German general staff for the purpose of inciting civil war and of demoralizing the Russian armies. In these circumstances there arose among Western statesmen the natural hope that somehow a great Russian leader would arise around whom the "sane" elements would rally in relief of the stricken nation. Since the Allies were terrified about the consequences of Russian withdrawal from the conflict they placed great faith in this idea. Thus neither the United States nor her Allies extended recognition to the new Russian government. There were, however, differences of opinion as to how Bolshevik Russia should be treated. Naturally the immediate objective of the Allies was to keep her in the war. Some Allied representatives encouraged revolutionary groups to overthrow the Bolsheviks and reestablish the Eastern front, while others conferred with Bolshevik leaders and intimated a promise of Allied support if Russia continued in the war against Germany.

President Wilson's attitude appeared to be ambivalent. While he strongly opposed recognition of the Bolshevik regime, he expressed in the sixth of his Fourteen Points an official attitude which demanded for Russia the free and unembarrassed opportunity of determining her own future without pressure or intervention from her Allies. Moreover, he pointed out that the treatment accorded to Russia during this critical period would be the "acid test" of Allied good will and understanding of Russia's needs as distinguished from their own self-interest. The Allies, anxious to rally the Russians against Germany and to prevent great quantities of munitions from falling into the hands of the Central Powers, were unable to convince Wilson of the military necessity for intervention in Russia. Despite repeated and impassioned requests, President Wilson remained adamant for six months. Then in the face of what appeared to be new and compelling circumstances, he changed his mind. He not only agreed to intervention in North Russia, but he took the lead in inviting the Japanese to participate in a joint intervention in Siberia.

The President's motives have been hotly debated by scholars. Some have attributed American policy primarily to anti-Bolshevik feeling and the desire to overthrow Lenin's regime. Others have viewed American efforts as inspired by the hope of rescuing some 50,000 loyal Czecho-Slovaks fighting their way eastward across Siberia against an exaggerated horde of Austro-German prisoners-of-war. Wilson's policy has also been explained as an attempt to thwart Japanese imperialism in eastern Siberia and northern Manchuria and to protect America's traditional open-door policy. Others have seen intervention as directed basically against Kaiserism itself in the shape of both the Austro-German prisoners-of-war and the Bolsheviks, whom the President mistakenly regarded as German agents.

Certain diplomatic historians have assessed Wilson's decision as stemming from intense Allied pressure and the wish to maintain a cooperative stance with his allies even though disagreeing with their rationale for intervention. At least one historian has interpreted Wilson's intervention policy as growing out of a desire to support Russian rational liberal-nationalism against what he envisaged as the interrelated threats posed by German imperialism and Russian Bolshevism. Finally, various combinations and modifications of the preceding explanations have been supported by historians in the endeavor to disentangle the complexities of the decision-making process in regard to Russian intervention. Whatever may have been the initial reasons for intervention, American troops remained in Russia until 1920.

The readings which follow are divided into three main sections. The first is designed to provide both the general and more specific background of United States relations with Russia and Japan from 1917 to 1920. The second section includes selected pertinent documents significant for an examination of the development of American decisions regarding the Bolshevik revolution, intervention, and the Russian Civil War itself. The final section presents a group of historical interpretations which offer diverse and conflicting explanations of some of the critical decisions made by the United States toward the Bolsheviks in this crucial period.

Wilson's entire Russian policy has been the subject of varying degrees of both praise and disapproval. The issues involved are vital not only in relation to Bolshevik Russia at the close of World War I but also in regard to Communist China following World War II and the American involvement in Viet Nam to-day. Why did the United States refuse to recognize the Bolshevik government? Was non-recognition a wise policy? What, in fact, did it seek to achieve? If appropriate aid had been offered to Russia, could she have been persuaded to remain in the war against Germany? After enunciating his belief in Russia's right to self-determination and his own opposition to intervention, why did Wilson change his mind? Why, indeed, were American troops sent to Russia? Was American intervention basically anti-Bolshevik in character? Was it anti-Japanese? Was it anti-German? Was it really designed to rescue the Czechs? If intervention was basically anti-German, anti-Japanese, or anti-Bolshevik, why didn't Wilson forthrightly say so? Why did Wilson finally decide to invite only the Japanese and not his other Allies to participate in the Siberian expedition? Why were American troops unable to "rescue" the Czechs from Russia immediately at the close of World War I? If the United States had been initially deceived either about the menace of German and Austrian war prisoners or about the plight of the Czecho-Slovaks, why were American troops not then withdrawn from Russia? Indeed, why were they not sent home after the Armistice? Why did Wilson finally decide to aid Admiral Kolchak, a man in whom he admittedly did not believe? Why were American troops kept in Russia until 1920? If the attitude of the American State Department had indeed ceased to be neutral, why were American troops not maintained and reinforced? Why were they not ordered to fight against the Bolsheviks in Siberia? Why were American troops finally withdrawn? Did American policy during the Russian Civil War achieve its objectives? Why did Wilson's policy appear to be so confused and ineffectual? Why did it appear to be so much at variance with the principles which he had enunciated in his Fourteen Points? Finally, what lessons are to be learned for the present in this first American attempt to cope with the problems raised by a Communist revolution? [NOTE: Footnotes in the selections have been omitted for reasons of space.]

CONTENTS

III. CONFLICTING INTERPRETATIONS

THE CLASH OF ISSUES

Why did President Wilson agree to intervention in Russia?
. . . [B]y the end of January, 1918, President Wilson had accepted . . . a decision to implement a policy designed to support counter-revolution against the Soviet Government. WILLIAM A. WILLIAMS.

Thus the plight of the Czechs as he [Wilson] understood it appealed to him, and he thought he saw at long last a possibility for putting an end to the pressures of the British and French for action in Siberia without associating himself with their political schemes, of which he was deeply suspicious. . . . [T]here is no suggestion more preposterous than that he was animated in these decisions by hostility toward the Russian people or by a desire to overthrow the Soviet regime with American forces. GEORGE F. KENNAN.

Having witnessed the penetration of Japanese imperialism on the mainland of Asia between 1914 and 1917, Washington had no illusions concerning the true intentions of Tokyo in Siberia. . . . The necessity to stop the Japanese drive for empire was accordingly imperative. By virtue of war and revolution Soviet Russia became the scene of the battle, and the United States emerged as the defender of Russian sovereignty in the Far East. PAULINE F. TOMPKINS.

What could not possibly be defended was what was actually done — sending in an army to meet an imaginary enemy. Intervention made sense, as the administration conceived of it, only if one assumed that the Bolsheviks were German agents and that they had given arms to the German and Austrian prisoners of war so that the Central Empires could take over Siberia. None of these things happened to be true. The whole business rested on an illusion of staggering proportions.

CHRISTOPHER LASCH.

In the Far East [the U.S.] purpose first and last was to resist the Japanese penetration of northern Manchuria and Siberia.

A. WHITNEY GRISWOLD.

What did American intervention achieve?
Despite the fiction of characterizing America's role as "Military Action," the fact remains that such action was intervention and as such was a deliberate interference in the internal affairs of the Russian people prolonging the Civil War and entailing untold loss of life and property.

WILLIAM S. GRAVES.

. . . [A]ctive intervention . . . enabled the Russian Communists to raise the cry of capitalist encirclement and call upon the patriotic citizens to repel the invader of Russian soil. . . . We were savagely condemned along with our associates. . . [O]ur actions merely served to intensify and justify a hatred that had existed before the beginning of the Communist experiment in Russia. THOMAS A. BAILEY.

. . . [I]t was justified by conditions as they appeared to be at the time, it refrained from militaristic adventures of its own, it restrained such adventures on the part of others, and it created a situation which made necessary the withdrawal of all Allied forces from Siberian soil when it was withdrawn, thus making impossible territorial conquests and acquisitions on Russian soil by other nations whose interests in the Far East might easily have induced them to take over the pacification, and ultimately for permanent colonial administration, vast areas of Russia's Far East.   NEWTON D. BAKER.

It may be repeated, however, that while giving in to the Allies upon the principal issue involved, our influence during these years did work as a somewhat moderating influence upon the more ambitious ideas they for a time held as to the extent to which intervention might be pushed. Yet this consideration cannot outweigh the fact that we followed a policy toward Russia in 1918 and 1919 that could hardly be reconciled with the democratic principles we professed, or with our declared intention to allow the Russian people to settle their own internal problems.

FOSTER RHEA DULLES.

I. HISTORICAL BACKGROUND

Thomas A. Bailey: DAYS THAT SHOOK THE WORLD

Thomas A. Bailey, American diplomatic historian and professor of American history at Stanford University, is the author of numerous books and articles and has written one of the few full-length surveys of Russian-American relations. The selection below emphasizes American attitudes toward diplomatic problems and delineates the evolution of American opinion toward Russia. Bailey presents in lively style American reactions toward the fall of Russian autocracy, the rise of the Provisional government, the victory of the Bolsheviks, and the Allied intervention and its aftermath.

WHEN war erupted in the summer of 1914 autocratic Russia, by virtue of binding alliances, found herself in the camp of the democracies, principally Britain and France, fighting militaristic Germany and Austria-Hungary.

The presence of despotic Russia in the democratic fold was greeted in the United States with mixed feelings. We were well aware that the semi-Oriental Russian absolutism, which claimed dominion over both body and soul, was perhaps the most oppressive in the western world. A few of us vaguely feared that in the event of an Allied victory a partly civilized and imperialistic Russia might be as dangerous as a victorious Germany. Had not the Czar contributed substantially to the coming of the current war by his ill-timed mobilization?

But American sympathies were overwhelmingly on the side of the western democracies, and autocratic Russia rose in respectability by keeping good company. The oft-heralded Slavic Peril, which had faded after the Russo-Japanese War, on the whole seemed tame when compared with the vibrant militarism, navalism, imperialism, and jingoism of Germany under Kaiser Wilhelm II. The long-moribund ancient friendship, submerged under decades of unpleasantness, was in some degree again revived. We were favorably impressed by Russia's contributions to the Allied cause, especially her self-sacrificing invasion of East Prussia, which diverted German troops from France on the eve of the battle of the Marne and probably saved Paris. The embattled British, who naturally embraced the traditionally hostile Russian a good deal more enthusiastically than did the neutral Americans, further colored our outlook by sending us news with a pro-Russian slant.

Nicholas II also improved his standing in the United States by interdicting, as a war measure, the sale of alcoholic liquor. Countless thousands of American prohibitionists rejoiced. If Alexander II in 1861 had freed over 20,000,000 serfs from the grip of their masters, Nicholas II in 1914 had freed some 160,000,000 people from the grip of demon vodka. What unen-

From Thomas A. Bailey, *America Faces Russia: Russian-American Relations from Early Times to Our Day* (Ithaca: Cornell University Press, 1950), pp. 228–250. Reprinted by permission of the author.

lightened Russia had done, enlightened America might also do.

American immigrants were likewise pleased by the prospect of a new day in Russia for persecuted minorities, even though there was no real faith in Czarist promises. "Russia has made pledges before and broken them," scoffed the Springfield *Republican.* Specifically, the Russian army issued a manifesto which rather vaguely held out hope of a re-united and self-governing Poland under Czarist auspices. The Jews were also assured of better treatment, which as it turned out was not satisfactorily forthcoming. Jewish-Americans, still flushed by their abrogation victory of 1911, were perhaps the one group in America most outstandingly anti-Russian, as a consequence of which they appeared to be, whether correctly or not, pro-German. The German-born Jewish banker, Jacob H. Schiff, declined to participate in a huge Allied loan, even though it would have brought substantial profits to his firm. The Russian officials were well aware of Jewish hostility and deeply resentful of it.

At the outset of the war the United States and Russia were drawn more closely together, especially by American exports. Partly to fill the vacuum caused by the withdrawal of German goods, and partly to supply some of the Czar's military needs, exports from America increased from some $27,000,000 annually to almost $500,000,000 in 1916 — a volume never previously attained, and not again to be attained until the lush days of lend-lease in the 1940's. Russian bonds, bearing a high interest rate indicative of the risk, were floated in the United States to the extent of some $86,000,000.

Yet unpleasant reports from the realm of the Romanovs continued to discolor this rather roseate picture. There were accounts of German agents and saboteurs, of bureaucratic stupidity and mismanagement, of Grand Ducal cowardice and bungling. After initial successes, the Russian armies were driven back by the Germans and yielded huge chunks of territory. As in the Russo-Japanese War, the American newspapers poked fun at this constant rearward motion, while expressing admiration for the Russian capacity to absorb punishment, lose enormous numbers of prisoners, and still keep up the fight. "About the only thing the Russians have consistently beaten during the war is a retreat," sneered the Philadelphia *North American* in 1915.

As additional disasters befell Czarist armies, it became evident that the stories were true about soldiers being sent into wintry combat without proper shoes, clothing, blankets, and even rifles. They were supposed to pick up arms and boots from fallen comrades, all of which pointed to continuing graft and incompetence. Other tales credited the ignorant and lecherous priest Rasputin with exercising a malign influence over the Czar and the Czarina. His assassination on the eve of the 1917 revolution caused many of our citizens to feel more kindly toward the Empire.

In March of 1917 the news reached the United States that Nicholas II, unable to stem the tide of revolution, had been forced to abdicate. A provisional government was formed and took steps toward long-awaited political and social reforms, such as freedom of assembly, extension of the suffrage, the abolition of restrictions on race and religion, and the granting of privileges to minorities, including independence for Poland and virtual independence for Finland. Tens of thousands of political exiles were reported streaming back from the mines of Siberia.

These momentous changes were greeted with genuine enthusiasm in the United States. Russian democracy had at long last broken through the hard crust of despotism — or so it seemed. The Romanovs were removed; perhaps the contagion would spread to the lànds of our potential enemies, Hohenzollern Germany and Hapsburg Austria-Hungary. "The Czar has abdicated. Next!" gloated the Philadelphia *Press*. Washington, after a wait of only a few days, hurriedly recognized the new provisional government — the first among the great powers to do so.

The satisfaction of our people, aside from their traditional devotion to democracy and hatred of monarchy, sprang partly from the imminence of our war with Germany. We had recently broken relations with Berlin and were about to embark upon a frenzied crusade to make the world safe for democracy. But our slogans would ring hollow if the blackest autocracy in the world were on our side. As if to prove that the United States was arrayed with righteousness, Providence (and the Russian revolutionists) removed this embarrassing incubus only three weeks before Congress formalized hostilities. In his war message President Wilson referred eloquently to the essential democracy of the Russian people, and to the Germanic character of their autocracy. "Here," he exulted, "is a fit partner for a League of Honour." We were now more than the friends we once had been; we were allies dedicated to a common cause.

American rejoicing was also inspired by the naïve supposition that Russia, now that she was a democracy, would continue the war with renewed zest. The purging of pro-German influences from the Czarist clique would eliminate an element that was inefficient, corrupt, disruptive, and treasonable. Democracies, knowing the ideals for which they fought, were, we fondly believed, invariably more determined fighters. We had actually little or no appreciation of the terrible sacrifices in blood and treasure that the Russian people had already been called upon to make.

Powerful and vocal groups of hyphenates in America were likewise overjoyed, especially the Jewish-Americans. Their anti-Russianism had brought down upon them vehement accusations of pro-Germanism, and now they could support the Allied cause wholeheartedly. Poles, Finns, and other racial minorities hailed the dawn of a new era, and hundreds of former Russian subjects began the long journey from the United States back to the Old Country. American businessmen talked optimistically of a revived commercial treaty; bankers spoke hopefully of new loans. All lovers of free worship gave thanks to their God, and even the Roman Catholics, with the apparent promise of a vast new field for their faith, were prepared to bury their age-old animus against the anti-Pope Czar and his schismatic Greek Orthodox Church.

The amateurish and purblind American ambassador in the Russian capital was a sixty-seven-year-old Missouri grain merchant by the name of David R. Francis. Lacking any real knowledge of Russia, he egregiously misled Washington as to the prospects of the provisional government. President Wilson, acting upon such misinformation, dispatched a special mission for the purpose of encouraging the Russians to keep up the fight. It was headed by the wealthy and conservative elder statesman Elihu Root, who was distasteful to the liberal and radical elements of Russia and who, repelled from intimate contact with them, could not bring back a full-length picture of what was happening. The new provisional government on its part sent a war mission to the United States. The visitors were enthusiastically received by both the House of Representatives and the Senate, and succeeded in persuading our government to advance some $187,000,000, none of which was ever repaid.

In the summer of 1917 the provisional government launched a new offensive against the Austro-German forces which, after early victories, collapsed miserably. The radicals meanwhile had been weakening the will of the masses to fight. Conspicuous among the agitators were Nicolai Lenin, whom the German High Command, hoping to produce dissension, had permitted to cross Germany from Switzerland in a sealed railway car, and Leon Trotsky, who had only recently been the editor of a radical sheet in New York City. The slogans of the Bolsheviks — "Loot the Looters," "No annexations, no indemnities," "Peace, Land, and Bread," and "All Power to the Soviets" — proved pervasively disruptive.

The lid blew off when, in November, 1917, the Bolsheviks seized power, with Lenin and Trotsky in leading roles, and with the virtually unknown Stalin in a secondary post. Sweeping changes were instituted, some more rapidly than others. The peasants were given the land (which was soon nationalized), and the workingmen were given control of the factories (which were later nationalized). Banks were nationalized and private accounts were seized. Churches and church property were confiscated, religious instruction in the schools was abolished, and God was exiled. The debts of the Empire and the provisional government were completely repudiated, partly as a gesture of defiance to bourgeois capitalism, although somewhat later the Bolsheviks indicated a willingness to discuss a mu-

tual scaling down of claims. Secret treaties were exhumed from the archives and published, in an effort to expose the wickedness of the Czar and his imperialistic allies.

The Bolshevik revolution burst upon the outside world with staggering force. Conservative and capitalistic America, repelled by even mild socialism, was scandalized by Communistic methods and programs. Wealthy Americans, dedicated to the sanctity of private property, were shocked by the brutal seizure of land, factories, and other agencies of production. Our bankers and taxpayers were alarmed by the cavalier repudiation of financial obligations, a considerable amount of which was held by American investors. Religionists were shocked by the fate of the churches, all the more so when lurid stories arrived relating how the "godless" Bolshevik "Jews" had enthroned atheism and turned temples of worship into houses of ill fame. The New York *Tribune* condemned the revolutionists as "embittered paranoiac adventurers," while a correspondent of the New York *Times* wrote of the "nightmare in a lunatic asylum." George Kennan, who had welcomed the March revolution, branded the Bolsheviks a "usurping gang," and soon was urging that we send troops to Russia to help overthrow the new despotism. Perhaps the only influential segment of the press that reacted sympathetically to the Bolshevik "democracy" was the Hearst chain, but for various reasons Hearst ultimately reversed himself and became one of the most implacable foes of the "Reds."

The Bolsheviks were not only a menace to capitalistic society but more immediately they were a threat to the success of what they condemned as the "imperialistic" war then being waged by the Allies. Almost simultaneously with the

Russian revolution, the Italian front began to collapse under the German-Austrian sledge hammer. If the Bolsheviks withdrew Russia from the conflict, thereby releasing several hundred thousand German veterans for the western front, the democracies might be overwhelmed. The vast resources of Russia would then be available to Germany, which would be able to prolong the struggle by billions of dollars and millions of lives. "The Bolsheviki," exclaimed the Houston *Chronicle*, "are as dangerous to organized government as are the Hohenzollerns and Hapsburgs, and probably more so."

Hostile though the American people were to the Bolshevik revolution, they were not so deeply interested as they should have been in these faraway and confused events. The belief was current in the United States that the usurpers were such violent extremists that they would soon kill themselves off with crazy ideas, and thus make room for a genuinely democratic growth. They were so negligible a minority — they *were* a minority — that they would soon fall from power. When the liberty-drunk Russian masses sobered down, their essential "democracy" would reassert itself and they would soon be back in the war. We did not think too kindly of the defunct provisional government anyhow. It had courted its own death by dealing too mildly with the radicals. It had been somewhat socialistic, and we were suspicious of socialists. "Socialism," remarked the Detroit *Journal* in 1919, "is Bolshevism with a shave."

The delusion was also current that the revolution had been cooked up by the German High Command, which was merely using Trotsky and Lenin as tools, and as a result the whole Bolshevik edifice would soon collapse of its own weight. This partly explains why our press and people took so little notice of the sensational secret treaties, which our allies had earlier made with one another for dividing up the spoils of battle, and which the Bolsheviks had so rudely published. Was not this exposé only a German-Bolshevik hoax designed to sow dissension between us and our allies?

If the Washington government was deceived by the on-the-spot misrepresentations of Ambassador Francis, the American people were no less completely deceived by their own press. Our conservative newspapers deliberately or unconsciously slanted their news columns against the usurping regime. The New York *Times*, according to a study made by Walter Lippmann and Charles Merz for the period from November, 1917, to November, 1919, referred to the probable fall of the Bolsheviks no fewer than ninety-one times. If such was the practice of so distinguished a daily, one can well imagine the tactics of less reliable journals. In addition, anti-Bolshevik propaganda in the United States was being disseminated by disillusioned or conservative Russians, many of whom were traveling or remaining in America for their "health." Conspicuous among them was the orphaned Russian ambassador, whom we continued to recognize for more than five years after the fall of the provisional government.

The Washington administration cautiously withheld recognition from the Bolsheviks, in glaring contrast to its open-armed welcome of the March revolutionists. Wilson himself was a strong non-interventionist and self-determinist, and not unwilling to let the dust settle in the hope that a triumphant democracy would emerge. If one could assume, as many Americans did, that Leninism was but a passing phase, the United States would merely prejudice good relations with the succeeding government if it opened premature negotiations with the Bolsheviks.

Thus from the very beginning every instinct of our administration and people was to turn against the new gang of revolutionaries. The argument is now used, especially in Communist circles, that *because* of this unfriendliness the Bolsheviks *developed* a strong enmity for the United States. The fact is that even before the fugitive Lenin and other Communists reached prostrate Russia, they had in their writings and speeches declared ideological warfare on the capitalistic world, of which the United States was rapidly becoming the most powerful pillar. Before leaving New York to undo the provisional regime, Trotsky urged his followers to keep on organizing until they were able "to overthrow this damned rotten capitalistic government." All this was before Washington had an opportunity to declare itself, or to support counterrevolutionary movements.

In December, 1917 — a month after the Bolsheviks seized power — the new Communist clique appropriated 2,000,000 rubles for the use of its agents abroad in promoting world revolution. In other ways — and many months before American armed intervention — the Bolshevik directorate proclaimed its undying hostility to the decadent capitalistic world. Significantly in 1919, less than two years after the Leninist coup in Russia, the Communist party of the United States, with well-established Moscow connections, sprang into being. From such tiny seeds was destined to grow an enormous crop of ill will.

The Bolsheviks first sought a general armistice, and failing to secure one, attempted to withdraw from the war singlehandedly. Unsuccessful in this also, they were finally compelled at bayonet point, in March, 1918, to sign with Germany the humiliating treaty of Brest Litovsk, by which they lost about a fourth of their population and much of their most valuable territory.

The Allies and the United States, left to continue the conflict alone, were shocked and angered by what they regarded as an act of perfidy. The legend took quick root, in ignorance of their immense sacrifices, that the Russians were cowardly quitters. "Trotsky might get the ignoble peace prize," jeered the Raleigh (North Carolina) *News and Observer*. Hearst's Baltimore *American* castigated the work of "a group of lewd fellows of the baser sort: filthy pocket-pickers and despicable degenerates of lucre." With a strong suggestion of sour grapes, the Kansas City *Star* rationalized: "Well, if Russia is lost to us, all right. We never did want to make the world safe for the Bolshevik kind of democracy anyway."

American public opinion warmly supported the decision of President Wilson neither to recognize nor to have dealings with the Bolsheviks. We still sympathized with the unfortunate Russian people, and there was some little demand for armed intervention to help them throw from their backs this new and more terrible tyranny. We were also neck-deep in a desperate war with Germany, and since relations with Moscow were secondary to victory, we were under strong compulsion to assist the counter-revolutionists in the hope of keeping Russia in the conflict. At all costs those powerful German divisions had to be pinned down on the eastern front. A few Americans even entertained the thought that we might have to fight a second conflict, once we had disposed of the Kaiser, this time to make the world safe against Bolshevism.

After the surrender at Brest Litovsk,

the confusion in Russia thickened. There were separatist movements on the periphery, civil wars within (Reds versus Whites), interventions from without, and assaults on the flanks, including invasion from Turkey. The central core of the nation was attacked from every point of the compass: north, south, east, and west. At one time, when Bolshevik fortunes were at lowest ebb, Russia was reduced to approximately the size of medieval Muscovy.

From the north an Allied expedition operating out of Archangel marched to within some 400 miles of Moscow (January, 1919). From the east (Siberia) a White army under Admiral Kolchak came within some 500 miles of Moscow (May, 1919); from the south a White force under General Denikin advanced to within about 175 miles of Moscow (October, 1919); and from the west a White detachment under General Yudenich penetrated to a point seven miles from Petrograd (October, 1919). This complicated picture does not take into account the subsequent invasion by Poland from the west or that by the White General Wrangel from the south.

Two of these foreign interventions involved the United States. An Allied expedition occupied Murmansk and Archangel, in northern Russia on the Arctic Ocean, in the summer of 1918. The primary objectives were initially to encourage local resistance to the Germans and to keep huge quantities of military supplies from falling into German hands. Later the invaders co-operated with the counterrevolutionaries (Whites) against the Bolsheviks (Reds), thereby drawing upon themselves the wrath of Moscow.

The United States contributed some 5,000 troops to the Archangel intervention, upon assurances that they were to guard military stores and to render such aid as was acceptable to the Russian people without interference in their internal affairs. The American press at the outset seems to have been rather favorable to the enterprise, although some fear was expressed that a foreign invader would rally the people behind the Bolsheviks. But armed support of the Whites inevitably led to clashes with the Reds, in which American boys lost their lives. A regiment from Michigan was frozen in at Archangel, and the confused doughboys sent home "gripe" letters, some of which were published in the local newspapers. One of them wrote:

It's the land of the infernal odor,
The land of the national smell,
The average United States soldier
Would rather be quartered in L.

The United States had gone to war to fight Germany, not the Bolsheviks, and indignation meetings were held in Michigan against Wilson's undeclared and unauthorized war in North Russia. The junior United States Senator from Michigan, Charles E. Townsend, reported that he was receiving hundreds of letters and telegrams from outraged parents. Following a minor mutiny and other difficulties, the American troops were finally withdrawn, in July, 1919, after having suffered more than 500 casualties. The Allies felt betrayed, the Bolsheviks were embittered, and the Americans were bewildered.

Wilsonian intervention in Siberia was undertaken on a considerably larger scale and involved about 9,000 United States troops. For the ostensible purpose of rescuing a marooned contingent of some 45,000 Czecho-Slovak soldiers who could be used in France, as well as keeping military supplies from falling into Bolshevik hands, a joint Allied intervention was undertaken in 1918. Wilson joined the enterprise with extreme reluctance, and primarily for the purpose of restraining the Japanese, who were clearly taking advantage of the European conflict to promote their imperialistic ambitions at the expense of Russia.

Strange as it may seem, the ill-starred Siberian expedition received considerable public support in the United States. For one thing, the unfortunate Czechs, who had many cousins in the United States, caught the popular fancy. Some Americans actually criticized the administration for not starting sooner, on a larger scale, and with less ambiguous objectives.

Determined though Wilson was not to side with the Whites against the Reds, American troops were gradually sucked into the morass. One of our main objectives was to protect the trans-Siberian railroad, in the interests of succoring the Czechs, but keeping open this line meant that we were ensuring supplies for the White Admial Kolchak, who was the most serious threat to Red Moscow. Bolshevik bands attacked American guards, killing thirty-six, and the guards shot back. The Reds were angry because we were indirectly helping their enemies; the Whites were bitter because we did not help enough; the Allies were displeased because we had such limited objectives; and the Japanese were suspicious because we so obviously were trying to hamper their ambitions. Actually, by opposing Japanese designs we were promoting the territorial integrity of Russia.

After the Allied Armistice with Germany in November, 1918, the Siberian expedition simply failed to make sense. The Czechs had been evacuated; military supplies could no longer help the Germans. Why continue to fight unknown enemies for unrevealed reasons? The parents of the American boys, who had been drafted for other purposes, brought great pressure to bear on their representatives in Congress to bring the lads home. Republican partisans, who were accelerating the postwar drift toward isolation, lambasted the Democratic Woodrow Wilson for his unconstitutional private war. The last American contingent was withdrawn from Siberia in 1920, while a Japanese band, reflecting the satisfaction of the Tokyo imperialists, played, "Hard Times Come Again No More."

The objectives of the United States in the Archangel and Siberian expeditions were not avowedly anti-Bolshevik. But in the case of Admiral Kolchak, whom the Allies backed as the principal White hope, the story was different. After extracting pledges from him that he would work for the freedom of the Russian people and recognize foreign debts, Wilson joined the Allies in a program of economic support and military supplies for Kolchak. The United States also co-operated with the Allies in sending food and munitions to the Poles during their war with Russia in 1920.

Wilson's unofficial and backhanded clashes with the Bolsheviks weaken the allegation that Russia is the one great power with which we have never had an armed conflict. Some American newspaper editors freely stated that by participating in intervention we were actually waging war on the Bolsheviks. Spokesmen for the new revolutionary government were not backward about echoing the same charges.

At all events, the active intervention of the Allies, rather feebly seconded by the United States, enabled the Russian Communists to raise the cry of capitalistic encirclement, and call upon patriotic citizens to repel the invader of Russian soil.

Fearful that imprisoned Nicholas II would be released by the foreign-supported White invaders, the Bolsheviks cold-bloodedly murdered him and his family in July, 1918. His death caused no great sorrow in the United States, where we have usually applauded the abrupt termination of royal dynasties. Yet if we were indifferent to the passing of Nicholas II, the Bolsheviks were not indifferent to the armed intervention of the Allies and the United States. We were savagely condemned, along with our associates. But both we and our comrades in arms had already been liberally condemned before becoming involved in any of these dubious enterprises, and our actions merely served to intensify and justify a hatred that had existed before the beginning of the Communist experiment in Russia.

In August, 1918, a female revolutionist wounded Lenin with her revolver and touched off the full-blown Red Terror, which was accelerated by the nervous tension resulting from beleaguered Russia's desperate plight. Hundreds of persons, chiefly from the upper and middle classes, were done to death. Kill a thousand today, ran the Bolshevist philosophy, so as to ensure the happiness of thousands tomorrow. Lurid reports reaching America told of streets running with blood and of a new electrically driven guillotine capable of decapitating 500 persons an hour. A corresponding White Terror accounted for the butchering of uncounted Bolshevik adherents, but American prejudices were so violently anti-Red that little account was taken of these atrocities, even when they were mentioned in our conservative press, which they often were not.

At the Paris Peace Conference in 1919 Wilson sought to secure Russian representation, but no agreement could be reached as to what faction represented the entire nation. Still wedded to nonintervention, Wilson resolutely resisted French and other schemes to crush what Winston Churchill called "the foul baboonery of Bolshevism." Wilson himself finally came to believe that the new dictatorship in Russia was just as selfish, ruthless, and pitiless as that of the Czars, but his heart went out to the ill-starred masses. He did co-operate with the Allied blockade against the Bolsheviks to the extent of an embargo, which appears to have commanded public support in America and which was not substantially lifted until 1920. This, in a very real sense, was waging economic war on Bolshevist Russia. . . .

Fear of Bolshevism among patriotic Americans found a spectacular outlet in the Great Red Scare of 1919. An epidemic of strikes then sweeping the country, many of them the natural result of skyrocketing prices, was commonly referred to as Moscow-inspired, especially the spectacular outbursts in Seattle and Boston. In the spring of 1919, while Hungary was going Bolshevik, a number of packages containing infernal machines were discovered in the New York post office bearing the addresses of prominent personages, and subsequently a series of explosions occurred in different cities, including a blast that wrecked both the home and nerves of Attorney General Palmer. This official, known as the "Fighting Quaker," undertook vigorous repressive measures, which included exclusion of a Socialist newspaper from the mails. "Too many persons in this country are enjoying the right of free screech," agreed the Brooklyn *Eagle*.

Most conspicuous of Palmer's activities was the rounding up of hundreds of so-called Reds. A popular song caught the spirit of the hour, "If you don't like your Uncle Sammy, then go back to your home over sea." In 1919 a total of 249 undesirables were loaded onto an American transport, satirically known as the "Soviet Ark," and bundled off to the Russian "paradise." Prominent among them were the veteran anarchists Emma Goldman and Alexander Berkman, who added notoriety to what one newspaper called the "unholiest cargo that ever left our shores." Enthusiastically applauding the "deportation delirium," Guy Empey wrote, "My motto for the Reds is S.O.S. — ship or shoot. I believe we should place them all on a ship of stone, with sails of lead, and that their first stopping place should be hell."

One prospective deportee was an emissary from the Soviet government, L. C. A. K. Martens by name, who had established offices in New York City for the ostensible purpose of opening trade relations. Snubbed by Washington, he issued statements designed to paint a more roseate picture of Russia, as a consequence of which he was accused of disseminating Communist propaganda. In imminent danger of deportation following an adverse ruling in December, 1920, he left voluntarily rather than involuntarily. (His experience in some respects was even less pleasant than that of Francis Dana at St. Petersburg, 1781–1783.)

The Red Scare was primarily a domestic disease, and more important as a manifestation of the overwrought emotionalism of the war than as an incident in Russian-American relations. But it further seared into the American public mind the familiar stereotype of a bloodthirsty, bewhiskered, bomb-throwing, free-loving Bolshevik.

The position of the Wilson administration, as emphatically set forth in a note by Secretary of State Colby, was that the United States would have no official traffic with the Communist regime. Though a minority, they had usurped and destroyed popular government. They had repudiated their lawful debts. Openly boasting of bad faith as an instrument of national policy, they were not only a menace to our institutions but to law, order, and the sanctity of international dealings. They were committed to unceasing international propaganda for world revolution through their diplomatic establishments, and also through the subterfuge of the Comintern. Such was the pronouncement of Secretary Colby in 1920.

Foster Rhea Dulles: THE BOLSHEVIKI MAKE PEACE

Volumes on the China trade, American-Japanese relations, and America's role in the Pacific have contributed to the reputation of Foster Rhea Dulles as an authority in the field of American foreign relations. The Road to Teheran presents a survey of America's historic relationship with Russia. The selection below offers an account of America's early relations with Bolshevik Russia based upon official, published sources.

From Foster Rhea Dulles, *The Road to Teheran*, pp. 113–128, copyright, 1944, by Princeton University Press. Reprinted by permission of Princeton University Press.

THE BOLSHEVIK revolution of November 1917 ushered in years of the utmost confusion. The economic collapse of a nation, foreign war and bitter civil strife, blockade and famine, the Red Terror, widespread suffering, misery and death would all be endured before great Russia again achieved anything like stability. And throughout these critical years foreign nations, including the United States, watched in uncertainty and with divided counsels, in appalling ignorance of what was really happening, the unfolding of a terrible drama.

The immediate reaction to the Bolsheviki's assumption of power was everywhere one of stunned and horrified surprise. For the American ambassador at Petrograd these feelings were mitigated only by the reassuring conviction, which he never lost, that the Reds could not possibly remain in control of the government. Francis wrote Consul General Summers in Moscow on November 8 that it was reported that the Petrograd Soviet had named a new cabinet with Lenin as Premier and Trotsky as Foreign Minister — "Disgusting! — but I hope such effort will be made as the more ridiculous the situation, the sooner the remedy."

His reports to Washington constantly reiterated his view that the new regime would not last and that the forces of democracy, so much more representative of the Russian people, would quickly reassert themselves. When the Bolsheviki did create a Council of People's Commissars, with Lenin as Premier and Trotsky as Commissar of Foreign Affairs, he dismissed it as an aberration. In striking contrast to his plea for immediate recognition of the government set up during the March revolution, Francis urgently advised that no action whatsoever be taken until the situation righted itself and the Bolsheviki were driven out of office.

The United States followed this advice — it continued to follow it for sixteen years. Reports poured in from every quarter which tended to confirm the impressions of the American envoy. The Russian ambassador in Washington promptly repudiated the new Soviet government, and the ill-starred Admiral Kolchak, on a visit to the Pacific coast, added his voice to the chorus predicting Lenin's speedy downfall. And apart from the supposed instability of the new regime, there was every other reason why America should hesitate to extend recognition. The Bolsheviki had seized power to carry out a revolutionary program of expropriating the land, turning the factories over to the workingmen and concluding an immediate peace. How could the capitalist world, the nations engaged in war against Germany, accept the implications of this declared policy? Little wonder that Secretary Lansing cabled Francis — "This Government awaits further developments.". . .

As upon the occasion of the March revolution, the immediately vital issue presented by the triumph of the Bolsheviki was whether Russia would remain in the war. The collapse of the eastern front under the Kerensky government had already clearly shown that little could be expected from her, but it was now feared that a separate peace would not only release German armies for fighting on the western front but would make Russia's vast resources available for the German war machine. The refusal to recognize the Soviet government in November 1917 was due not so much to hostility to the Bolsheviki themselves, although it was already an important factor in the general picture, as it was to the general belief that such a step would end all possibility of some other government, which might be willing to prosecute the war, coming into power.

The attitude of the Bolsheviki did nothing to disabuse the United States and the Allies of their fears that Russia would withdraw from the war. Their drive for peace got under way at once. While President Wilson thundered that "any body of free men that compounds with the present German Government is compounding for its own destruction," Lenin and Trotsky officially proposed immediate negotiations to conclude a democratic peace without annexation or indemnities, and with full self-determination for all nations. While they were ready to conclude a separate treaty if necessary, they hoped it could be a general peace. But the Allies pointedly ignored their proposals. Peace negotiations at the close of 1917 meant defeat for the Allied cause.

President Wilson first indicated the mounting concern over this problem in his annual message to Congress in December. The disclosure by Trotsky of the secret treaties whereby the Allies had agreed to divide up the spoils of war, disposing of the German colonies and making other territorial adjustments that ran directly counter to their professed aims, gave rise to the charge that imperialist ambition alone accounted for the prolongation of hostilities. The President felt compelled to recognize the validity of the Bolsheviki's peace formula, if not the justice of their attacks upon the Allies. He declared that no annexations, no contributions, no punitive indemnities expressed "the instinctive judgment as to right of plain men everywhere." But this crude formula, he emphatically stated, was being used "by the masters of German intrigue to lead the people of Russia astray . . . in order that a premature peace might be brought about before autocracy has been taught its final and convincing lesson, and the people of the world put in control of their own destinies."

His words had little effect in Russia. The Soviet leaders in Petrograd were determined upon peace and believed that the peoples throughout the world, including those of Germany, would rally to their support. "The American President Wilson, adopting the tone of a Quaker preacher," a government-inspired editorial in *Izvestia* declared, "reads to the people a sermon on the higher practical morality. The people know that Americans came into the war, not in the interests of right and justice, but because of the cynical interests of the New York Stock Exchange."

Instructions had been given by Lansing to American diplomatic agents to have no communications whatsoever with the agents of the Soviet government. Ambassador Francis' belief that Lenin and Trotsky were reckless adventurers, in German pay and acting under orders from the German General Staff, carried great weight with the State Department. Other Americans in Petrograd, however, began to wonder whether our policy was not the most effective means of ensuring the Bolsheviki's complete capitulation to Germany. Edgar Sisson, who had arrived on the scene as agent of the Creel Committee, confidentially cabled Washington that unless constructive action was taken Russia would soon have to be counted wholly out of the war, and that the American ambassador appeared "without policy except anger at Bolsheviks. . . ." There were reports from both Colonel Raymond Robins, now head of the American Red Cross, and Jerome Davis, supervisor of Y.M.C.A. activities, that the strength and stability of the Soviet government could no longer be denied. The American military attaché actually saw Trotsky and assured him, unofficially, that the United States had no intention of interfering in Russia's internal affairs and that "the time of protests and threats to the Soviet Government has passed, if that time ever existed." By the end of December even Francis himself tentatively suggested entering into relations with the Bolshevik regime, possibly recognizing as well an independent Ukraine and Siberia, in an attempt to keep Russia at least neutral. It would be "exceedingly distasteful," he cabled home, but he felt that it might be advisable.

Secretary Lansing refused to consider any such change of policy. As early as December 10 he had warned President Wilson that Bolshevik domination meant Russia's withdrawal from the war, expressing the further opinion that the only hope for the Allies was the rise of a military dictatorship. His candidate was General Kaledin of the Don Cossacks. While hesitating to support him openly — "because of the attitude which it seems advisable to take with the Petrograd authorities" — he cabled our embassy in London proposing an indirect loan to Kaledin's forces through the British or French governments. "I need not impress upon you," he concluded these instructions, "the necessity of acting expeditiously and impressing those with whom you talk of the importance of avoiding it being known that the United States is considering showing sympathy for the Kaledin movement, much less of providing financial assistance." With such ideas foreshadowing the interventionist policy of a later day, the Secretary of State naturally had no sympathy for any move that might strengthen the Bolsheviki.

A sharp rebuke was administered to Sisson for his interference with diplomatic affairs, our military attaché was recalled and Ambassador Francis was distinctly instructed to follow the policy that he had himself originally advised. There would be no further consideration, even indirectly or distantly, of recognizing the Soviet government. Lansing declared that it was "a despotic oligarchy as menacing to liberty as any absolute monarch on earth." To reply to its suggestions in regard to peace, "would be contrary to the dignity of the United States."

The refusal of the United States, in common with the Allied powers, to recognize their government or accept their peace proposals did not deter the Bolsheviki from entering into direct contact with Germany. Envoys of the two governments met early in December and concluded an armistice. But Trotsky's goal remained a general peace — not merely a Russian-German peace. He repeatedly called upon the Allies to participate in the negotiations being held at Brest-Litovsk, twice postponing them to allow the Allies the opportunity to send delegates. When they continued to disregard all such appeals, he tried to arouse the people of the world to take action into their own hands. "If the Allied Governments in the blind stubbornness which characterizes decadent and perishing classes," he declared in a ringing manifesto on December 29, "once more refuse to participate in the negotiations, then the working class will be confronted with the iron necessity of tearing the power out of the hands of those who cannot or will not give peace to the nations. . . ."

While the Allies stood fast in their refusal to enter into any peace parleys, the attacks of the Bolsheviki on the sincerity of their war aims could not be disregarded. Liberal elements in the United States and throughout western Europe, disturbed by the revelations of the secret treaties, were questioning the idealistic basis of the war as a crusade for democratic rights. Both Prime Minister Lloyd George of Great Britain and President

Wilson felt compelled to answer these doubters, and to meet the challenge of what the latter declared to be a voice "more thrilling and more compelling than any of the moving voices with which the troubled air of the world is filled . . . the voice of the Russian people." Insofar as the United States was concerned, a clarifying statement on war aims was also strongly urged from Petrograd by Edgar Sisson as a direct means of countering the Bolshevik peace propaganda among Russian workers and soldiers. It should be brief, Sisson advised, "in short, almost placard paragraphs, short sentences," and in such form that he could distribute it throughout the country and also send it across the German lines into enemy territory.

An answer to these appeals was the Fourteen Points, presented to the world on January 8, 1918, in the President's special message to Congress. It reflected neither animosity toward the Soviet government nor criticism of its leaders. At the time Wilson believed the negotiations at Brest-Litovsk had been permanently suspended. He was ready to accept the principles underlying Lenin and Trotsky's peace proposals, declaring it to be his heartfelt desire that some way could be found to assist the people of Russia in attaining their hope of liberty and ordered peace. "Their conception of what is right, of what is humane and honorable for them to accept," the President said, "has been stated with a frankness, a largeness of view, a generosity of spirit, and a universal human sympathy which must challenge the admiration of every friend of mankind. . . ."

The Fourteen Points themselves were an attempt to demonstrate that the United States was prepared to go even further than the Bolsheviki in projecting a liberal program for the future peace.

Article Six referred directly to Russia. It demanded as one of the basic terms of peace the complete evacuation of all Russian territory and settlement of the problem of Russia on a basis that would both assure her an unembarrassed opportunity for the determination of her own national policy and a sincere welcome into the society of free nations under institutions of her own choosing. "The treatment accorded to Russia by her sister nations in the months to come," Wilson solemnly asserted, "will be the acid test of their goodwill, of their comprehension of her needs as distinguished from their own interests, and of their intelligent and unselfish sympathy."

The fear that Russia might make a separate peace, or even join forces with Germany, was becoming a nightmare. Wilson was more and more persuaded that no stone should be left unturned in trying to win her further support for the Allied cause. This is not to impugn the idealism underlying the Fourteen Points. The President was expressing a world-wide desire for a peace that would in reality make the world safe for democracy and end all wars. His address nevertheless had the immediate and highly practical objective of countering Bolshevik propaganda. For he again insisted that the democratic peace that was the common objective of the Russian and American people could not be concluded until the world was assured that Germany's spokesmen were really speaking for the German people, and not for a military party whose creed was imperial domination. In other words, the proposed negotiations at Brest-Litovsk could achieve no real purpose because the complete overthrow of German tyranny was an absolute requisite to any satisfactory settlement of world problems.

The speech was at once widely distributed throughout Russia. Hundreds of thousands of pamphlets were printed; posters and placards pasted up in cities, towns and hamlets; newspapers everywhere prevailed upon to publish it. In all, more than three and one half million copies, one million in German, were sent out from Petrograd and Moscow through the agency of the Creel Committee. For a brief time it appeared that the Fourteen Points might actually have some effect on Russian policy. Although the suspended negotiations at Brest-Litovsk were renewed, the Soviet delegates refused to accept the harsh terms Germany proposed. She demanded Russia's surrender of the Baltic provinces, Poland and the Ukraine, where nominally independent governments were to be set up under German control. Disappointed and discouraged over the failure of the peoples of the world to back up his peace program, Trotsky bitterly attacked German imperialism. "We did not overthrow the Czar," he declared, "in order to fall on our knees before the Kaiser and beg for peace."

As the Kaiser's forces advanced toward Petrograd itself, there was for a time confusion in the ranks of the Bolsheviki as to the policy they should pursue. Lenin's single-minded goal was to save the revolution. He had favored peace on almost any terms. Now he hesitated in view of the brutally aggressive nature of the German demands. If there was any chance of obtaining effective aid from the Allies in defending Russia against the immediate enemy, he was ready to make a deal with them. Over against the opposition of those Bolshevik leaders who would have refused to traffic with any of the imperialist governments and favored a revolutionary war against all comers, the possibilities of such assistance were consequently explored. Was there any chance

of it? Colonel Robins, acting as an unofficial envoy between the American embassy and the Soviet government, tried to assure Trotsky that substantial aid would be forthcoming if the Russian army took up the fight. But his assurances could not take any concrete form.

"Colonel Robins," Trotsky said one time, as later reported by the Red Cross official, "your embassy sends you here with a big bag marked 'American help.' You arrive every day, and you bring the bag into my room, and you set it down by your chair, and you keep reaching into it as you talk, and it is a powerful bag. But nothing comes out."

It was an ironic situation. But however strongly the Allies and the United States desired to have Russia remain in the war, the events of the past few weeks had convinced them both that there was little possibility of this so long as the Bolsheviki remained in power. The American public, indeed, was becoming more and more distrustful of the Soviet government every day, and more embittered against the policies it was pursuing. A constituent assembly had met only to be immediately dissolved when the Bolsheviki found themselves in a minority among its elected representatives. The program of property expropriation had been further carried forward with the repudiation of all foreign debts. Increasingly alarming rumors were reaching the outside world of internal disturbance and revolt, and of the bloody methods being employed to suppress all political opposition to Soviet rule. And early in February, Ambassador Francis reported that he had conclusive documentary evidence confirming his belief that Lenin and Trotsky were in Germany's pay. These documents would in time be generally discredited. The American ambassador's basic assumptions were shown by events to be unwarranted. But the opinion was nevertheless almost universal in these decisive days that the Bolsheviki were merely the tools of imperial Germany.

Under such circumstances there was little disposition to aid the Soviet government even if the means had been available. It was felt that to do so, or even to recognize it, would be playing into Germany's hands. Wilson and Lansing were fully agreed that support for Russia would actually mean support for the Central Powers. And the wish constantly remained father to the thought: the days of the Bolsheviki were numbered. Support for a government on the verge of collapse would have highly unfortunate consequences, it was believed, and embarrass relations with any rival faction sincerely disposed to continue the war.

With the complete demoralization of their own armies and no effective foreign aid forthcoming, the Bolsheviki reluctantly decided, after a close vote in the Central Committee, upon capitulation. Germany presented new terms even more drastic than those the Soviet delegation had originally rejected, but on March 3, 1918, Russia nevertheless surrendered completely and signed the Treaty of Brest-Litovsk. She lost territory accounting for over a quarter of her total population, vast natural resources and a great part of her manufactures. "We declare openly before the workmen, peasants, and soldiers of Russia and Germany, and before the laboring and exploited masses of the whole," read the formal statement of the peace delegates, "that we are forced to accept the peace dictated by those who, at the moment, are more powerful, and that we are going to sign immediately the treaty presented to us as an ultimatum, but that at the same time we refuse to enter into any discussion of its terms."

Public opinion in America was shocked and horrified. "The signing of a formal peace on Germany's terms," the *New York World* declared, "marks the final act of betrayal on the part of the Bolsheviki. . . . Trotsky and Lenin have done their best by the Kaiser whether actuated by money, or lust for power, or the insanity of class hatred." Hardly anyone, however, questioned the almost universal belief that the Bolshevik leaders were agents of Germany. This was the easiest explanation for so catastrophic a development for the Allied cause. Colonel William B. Thompson, basing his opinion on his own experience in Petrograd, tried to point out that Lenin and Trotsky were not traitors but internationalists, seeking through any sacrifice to make possible the ultimate triumph of their utopian dreams of world peace. To desert Russia whatever the circumstances, he warned, might be disastrous. "Presently Russia must and will stabilize herself," Colonel Thompson wrote. "Shall she have the aid of the United States in working out her problems, or shall she be left to the ministrations of Germany?" Fear and distrust, for all the high promise of the sixth of Wilson's Fourteen Points, was all too clearly cutting off American sympathy.

The Bolsheviki made one more last desperate appeal to the Allies. Although convinced that it was of little use and that to hesitate much longer in concluding peace would be the death knell of the Soviet state, Lenin agreed to withhold ratification of the Brest-Litovsk treaty if any means could be found to resist further German aggression. Trotsky again made through Colonel Robins official inquiries as to what aid Russia might expect from the American government should she refuse even now to accede to the German demands and renew the war. But he was careful to make it clear, in a note forwarded to our embassy on March 5, that the Bolsheviki were quite as willing to surrender to the Germans as they were to accept any restrictive conditions from the Allies. His questions were conditioned, Trotsky declared, on the assumption "that the internal and foreign policies of the Soviet Government will continue to be directed in accord with the principles of international socialism."

President Wilson had already, in effect, answered the inquiries of the Russian government. In a message to the All-Russian Congress of Soviets on March 11, dispatched before Trotsky's delayed communication had been received in Washington, he redefined American policy. It was based upon sympathy and friendship for the Russian people, the President declared, and the United States would avail itself of every opportunity to secure for Russia complete sovereignty and independence in her own affairs. But he also stated that the United States was unhappily not in a position at the time to render the direct and effective aid to Russia that it might otherwise wish to extend.

Military and other considerations may have gone far toward justifying this position, but there was the further clear implication behind the President's words that the United States would have nothing to do with the Soviet regime. As already noted, the wavering policy of this country — and that of the other Allied governments — had steadied to the point of accepting a Russian-German peace as an inevitable consequence of the Bolsheviki's control of the Russian government. Nothing further could be done to check the German advance in Russia, it was felt, until the Bolsheviki were overthrown and some government set up in which the capitalist world could have real confidence.

The reaction of the Soviet Congress to this restatement of our policy was sharp and hostile. It struck back at once in adopting a resolution described by Acting Foreign Commissar Zinoviev as a slap in the face for President Wilson. The Congress took occasion to express its warmest sympathy for all peoples suffering from the horrors of an imperialist war, and declared its firm belief that the happy time was not far distant "when the laboring masses of all countries will throw off the yoke of capitalism and will establish a socialist state of society, which alone is capable of securing just and lasting peace, as well as the culture and well-being of all laboring people."

The growing bitterness of ideological conflict between Bolshevism and democracy was now heavily underscored. Nevertheless final action on the Brest-Litovsk treaty was once more postponed in the hope that some further reply to Trotsky's communication might still be forthcoming. For the Bolsheviki, despite the tone of Wilson's message, did not believe that America could afford to stand aloof in this international crisis. "The United States cannot permit Germany to become the autocratic master of dismembered Russia and especially of her markets," *Izvestia* declared. "The United States cannot in its own interest acquiesce in Germany's plan of turning Russia into a German colony. And it, unlike Germany, is not interested in establishing its political power in Russia. On the contrary, in view of its rivalry with Germany and Japan, the United States is directly interested to have Russia politically and economically strong and independent."

This had been our attitude in all our earlier relations with Russia; it would again in time become our policy. But *Izvestia* reckoned without American hostility toward the Bolsheviki and failed to realize how little confidence we had in their good faith. Just as Lenin believed that continued war would mean the collapse of the Soviet state, so was Wilson convinced that the triumph of Bolshevism spelled Russian surrender to Germany. Each was prepared to sacrifice everything else for his major goal. For Lenin war or peace was only an incident in the final triumph of the revolution, while for Wilson the revolution had its only real significance as it affected the defeat of Germany.

In any event no further message came from the United States upon the question of possible aid, and the Soviet Congress finally prepared to take definite action on the German treaty. Ratification had already been approved by the Central Executive Committee and Lenin was determined to force similar action through the Congress. Nevertheless Colonel Robins has told the story of how he was sitting on the steps near the platform during this critical meeting, when Lenin called him over and asked him what he had heard from his government. Colonel Robins answered, "Nothing." Having also received the same reply in regard to possible news from the British government, the Soviet leader then said: "I shall now speak for the peace. It will be ratified. . . ." This was on March 16, and that evening the final vote was taken. It was 784 in favor of ratification, 261 opposed. Russia was definitely and irrevocably out of the war.

Public opinion in the United States generally approved the resolution of the Wilson administration to have no traffic with the Bolsheviki. There was an occasional protest, such as that of Colonel Thompson, who felt our failure to accept the realities of the situation, however abhorrent Bolshevism might be to our capitalistic theories, had thrown Russia into Germany's arms. The press as a whole, however, did not see any alternative to the policy that had been adopted. The Bolsheviki had betrayed the Allied cause and threatened with their subversive propaganda the whole structure of the capitalist world. The reply of the Soviet Congress to President Wilson's expression of sympathy for the Russian people was generally interpreted, in the vehement characterization of Theodore Roosevelt, as a "mean and studied impertinence . . . a gratuitous and insulting expression for a class war in America."

In its official policy after Brest-Litovsk the United States continued to act upon the principle that the Soviet government did not have even *de facto* standing. The peace it had concluded with Germany consequently had no legal validity. Ambassador Francis remained in Russia, futilely trying to stem the Red tide sweeping over the country. He was constantly appealing to the Russian people to repudiate their leaders and disavow the peace treaty. In private correspondence he declared that should there be any movement along such lines, in whatever part of the country, he would try "to locate in that section and encourage the rebellion." Why did the Soviet government tolerate his presence under such circumstances? It at once clung to the hope that the United States would reverse its policy, and feared that the dismissal of the American ambassador might cause us to throw our support behind some one of the uprisings against Bolshevik authority.

There was a further ambiguity in the American position. In a statement on March 12, 1918 — that is, just prior to ratification of the Russian-German treaty — Acting Secretary of State Polk declared that the United States did not feel justified in regarding Russia as either an enemy or neutral power. Since she had in fact no government, and none of the acts of her so-called government could therefore be recognized, relations between Russia and America had in no way been altered by the events of the past few months. "The Government feels that it is of the utmost importance," Polk stated, "as affecting the whole public opinion of the world and giving proof of the utter good faith of all Governments associated against Germany, that we should continue to treat the Russians as in all respects our friends and allies against the common enemy."

What did such a policy involve? How could it be reconciled with actual conditions within Russia? Refusing to recognize or be friends with the Soviet government, we were irresistibly drawn into the role of foe. President Wilson had reiterated again and again that the United States had no intention of allowing itself to become involved in Russia's internal affairs. We would have no part in any war of factions. The willingness of the powers to let the Russian people work out their own destiny, he had declared, would be "the acid test" of their good will. But the fact that we were engaged in war with Germany, and that Russia under her Bolshevik rulers appeared to be swinging into the German camp, made such forbearance a seemingly impossible role. The pressure of events finally drove the United States to support an Allied program of intervention that was characterized by its open enmity to the Soviet government.

A. *Whitney Griswold:* WILSON CHALLENGES JAPAN

A. Whitney Griswold, who served Yale University as professor of history and later as president prior to his death in 1946, was a renowned specialist in Far Eastern affairs. Although written in 1938, prior to World War II, his book The Far Eastern Policy of the United States *is still regarded as a classic in its field. The selection below surveys America's response to the Russian Revolution within the context of America's traditional Far Eastern policy.*

WE HAVE SAID that in 1917 American diplomacy was preparing for the greatest offensive against Japanese expansion in its history. Not until the armistice lessened Wilson's preoccupation with Germany was he free to devote much energy to that offensive, which, when finally launched, took four principal forms: first, the effort to bind Japanese capital investment in China to the cooperative ordinances of the new four-power consortium; second, participation in the Allied military intervention of Siberia in order to prevent Japan from detaching the maritime provinces from Russian rule; third, insistence on the restoration of Shantung to China, and fourth, codification in treaty form of the principles of the Far Eastern policy of the United States together with the Wilsonian principles of non-aggression and collective security as applied to the Pacific Ocean and the region of Eastern Asia. The major parts of this progressively expanding program were accomplished at the peace conference and its sequel, the Washington Conference of 1921–1922. Organizing the consortium and the Siberian expedition began shortly after the conclusion of the Lansing-Ishii Agreement. The two were not unrelated, so far as the United States was concerned, for each constituted an American challenge to Japan's right to extend her political and economic influence onto the continent of Asia.

Wilson's decision in November, 1917, to permit the organization of a new four-power consortium was merely the curtain-raiser to an immensely complicated wrangle that lasted until October, 1920. Neither the President nor Lansing was finally reconciled to the impracticability of independent American loans until June, 1918. When they at last summoned the bankers to Washington, they found the latter in a recalcitrant mood. The greatly enlarged American banking group would accept Lansing's proposition only on two conditions: first, that it be assured of pooling its interests with the French, British and Japanese groups, in loans of a broadly international character, and second, that the United States Government announce that the loans were being made at its suggestion, a condition essential to their successful flotation on the American market. The government accepted these conditions. In so doing it assumed grave responsibilities toward the American investing public as well as toward the banking community. It virtually committed each to involvement in an international political contest the possible consequences of which, if it did not conceal, it certainly took no particular pains

to explain. The cardinal principles insisted on by the United States for the new consortium were that each national group should receive the active and exclusive support of its government; that all preferences and options in China held by the member banks should be pooled, and that the administrative integrity and independence of China should be respected. These principles collided sharply with Japan's well-known China program, as no doubt they were intended to do.

Prolonged Japanese-American negotiations ensued, in which Japan attempted to obtain the exclusion of Manchuria and Mongolia from the application of the consortium. To the Japanese way of thinking, the pooling of options and internationalization of loans in these regions were one and the same thing as the Knox neutralization scheme. And they were. The United States was once more clearly attempting by economic means to undermine Japan's economic monopolies in northeastern Asia, monopolies that rested on old and elaborate treaty structures involving French, British and Russian, as well as Chinese assent, and which, during 1918, Japan had expanded and strengthened through the medium of independent loans to the government of Tuan Chi-jui. Irrespective of the moral rights implicit in these treaties, they were, as we have repeatedly observed, effective political instruments. Japan was not inclined to throw them over at America's behest. A compromise was finally reached by which the United States assured Japan of its "good faith" that it and the other two consortium powers (France and England) would "refuse their countenance to any operation inimical to the vital interests of Japan." Japan thereupon submitted a bill of particulars, many of which were unacceptable to Great Britain and the United States. Only when the latter agreed to accept the South Manchuria Railway zone and a number of other specified railway projects and their related mining and industrial privileges in Manchuria and Mongolia as outside the scope of the consortium would Japan consent to join. This long economic contest, coinciding with the Siberian expedition and the peace conference contributed an acrimonious note to the more purely political questions at issue in the latter.

Military intervention in Siberia was the concluding, and for the United States perhaps the most serious, episode of the World War in the Far East. The background of this extraordinary venture was partly European, partly Far Eastern. In March and November, 1917, two great revolutionary spasms dislodged Russia from active participation in the war against Germany. Kerensky, the leader of the first revolution, tried to continue to co-operate with the Allies. With his downfall at the hands of the Bolsheviks, in the second revolution, the danger of a separate Russo-German peace became imminent. To forestall this, rally the White Russians to renew the fight against Germany, and prevent the latter from seizing Allied military stores in Russia, France and Great Britain early began to consider sending expeditionary forces into the Murmansk region of European Russia, and westward from Vladivostok into Siberia. When these projects materialized the United States participated in them with reluctance. It did not object to the Murmansk expedition as much as it did to the Siberian, however, as indicated by the fact that Wilson agreed to take part in the first over six weeks before he did in the second. Moreover, in the operations around Archangel, the United States did not adhere to any such rigid neutrality toward the Russian civil war as it did in Siberia. Since the announced purpose of both expeditions was the same, these discrepancies are enough to show that the American motives for taking part in each were different. In European Russia the United States was at first genuinely concerned with the protection of Allied military supplies and assisting the Russian elements that gave any evidence of wishing to fight Germany to do so. In the Far East its purpose first and last was to resist the Japanese penetration of northern Manchuria and Siberia.

The Russian Revolution instantly upset the *status quo* in the Far East and opened another field besides China and the German islands to Japanese expansion. Its immediate effect was to cause the breakdown of Russian control in northern Manchuria. This was an invitation to China as well as Japan, presenting the former an opportunity to reassert her sovereignty over the region. When the Bolsheviks seemed about to conquer it, the czarist Minister to Peking, though he represented a government that had long ignored China's sovereign rights in both Manchuria and Mongolia, suddenly remembered that "Russia had no territorial possessions in Manchuria" and urged the Chinese Government to send troops to co-operate with the local White Russian commander, General Horvat, against the Bolsheviks. The Allied Ministers to Peking did likewise, with the result that in December, 1917, Chinese troops intervened in the Russian civil war (albeit on nominally Chinese soil) on the side of the Whites. But China was not encouraged to carry her activities to the point of re-establishing her control over northern Manchuria. The Allies had no desire to see White Russia's rights there revert to China, nor to sponsor any further Chinese intervention in the Russian civil war. Great Britain warned the Chinese Government to this effect and the United

States, while recognizing "that China is entirely within her right in employing means to protect her sovereignty and territorial integrity," cautioned Peking against taking steps that might lead to armed conflict. Early in January, 1918, most of the Chinese troops were withdrawn and White Russian authority, in the person of General Horvat, was restored. From then on Chinese influence in Manchuria was a minus quantity. The province rapidly developed into a base for reactionary plots and military campaigns, financed and instigated by England, France and Japan, against the Bolsheviks over the border. This unneutral use of Chinese territory made it liable to invasion by the Soviet, and the possibility of Soviet attack served Japan as a convenient pretext for occupying it.

Japan had soon disclosed this intention. On January 17, 1918, Ambassador Morris reported from Tokyo that the Japanese Government had intimated its desire to undertake independently the occupation of Vladivostok and the operation of the Chinese Eastern and Amur Railways, should circumstances make these steps necessary. A few weeks later the British Government (which had been urging Wilson to consent to a Siberian expedition since the previous December) suggested to Washington that Japan be invited as the mandatory of the Allies to occupy the Trans-Siberian and Chinese Eastern Railways. Lansing promptly rejected the scheme, denying that intervention in Russia's affairs was warranted and maintaining that should it become necessary in the future, it should "be undertaken by international co-operation and not by any one power acting as the mandatory of the others." From this position the United States refused to budge. More than that, it insisted on placing the control and operation of the Chinese Eastern

Railway (that is, the part of the Trans-Siberian that ran through Manchuria) in the hands of its own railway corps that had been despatched to the Far East at the behest of Kerensky to manage the Trans-Siberian. Japan was not to be thwarted. In her secret treaty with Russia in 1916 she had arranged to take over a portion of the Chinese Eastern Railway in return for supplying Russia with war materials. To make sure that China would give her no trouble in this, she concluded two treaties with Peking (May 16 and 19, 1918) providing for Sino-Japanese military and naval co-operation in the event that their territories or "the general peace and tranquillity in the extreme Orient" should be menaced by the enemy.

The very month after the conclusion of these treaties, Japan was furnished the excuse for invoking them. Semenov, a cossack raider subsidized by England, France and Japan to prey on the Bolsheviks, was decisively defeated and retreated into Manchuria, his original base. His defeat was excitedly ascribed by his supporters to large numbers of freed German prisoners alleged to be swelling the ranks of the Red army. Late in July Japan, citing the danger of Bolshevik and German reprisals against the fugitive Semenov, invoked her military pacts with China and marched her troops into northern Manchuria. The eleventh-hour admonishment of Washington "that the American Government trusts that the Imperial Japanese Government shares its opinion that a military occupation of Manchuria would arouse deep resentment in Russia" and so "defeat the desire of the United States and Japan to aid in the rehabilitation of Russia and to re-enlist her people in the war against our common enemy" was ignored. Against the Franco-British support for Japan, and the influence Japan herself commanded over China, the United States could not prevail. For the time being all Manchuria was in Japanese hands. Washington therefore redoubled its efforts to prevent Japan from assuming independent control of the Chinese Eastern Railway. In this, though opposed as much by the British as by the Japanese, it finally scored a minor success. On January 9, 1919, an agreement was reached whereby the operation of the road was entrusted to an inter-Allied commission to be advised by a technical board headed by John F. Stevens, leader of the American railway corps in Siberia. The United States had not been able to prevent Japan from independently occupying Russian Manchuria, the realization of which failure may well have helped to reconcile Wilson to military intervention in Siberia.

Whether Japan, Great Britain or France first suggested an expedition to Siberia, it is certain that all three ardently espoused the idea and for six months brought every conceivable kind of pressure to bear on Wilson before they could obtain his consent to it. Not only that, but both England and France did their best to turn the whole expedition over to Japan as their mandatory, making it a co-operative enterprise only in deference to American policy. As early as December 1, 1917, Clemenceau was trying to convince Colonel House of the desirability of sending a Japanese expeditionary force into Siberia. On December 14, as Morris later reported to Washington, the British Ambassador in Tokyo, under specific instructions from London, broached the subject to the Japanese Foreign Office, leading Morris to conclude that "the initiative in the Siberian situation was taken by Great Britain and that prior to December 14 the Japanese Government had not seriously considered the question of intervention." On January 8 Lord Robert Cecil, Balfour's lieutenant in the Foreign Office, wrote his chief that,

The Japanese will not tell us what they intend to do, and are very angry if anyone else proposes to do anything. If they were not too unreasonable, the proper plan would undoubtedly be to land a force at Vladivostok to protect our stores there, *the force being in substance Japanese, with a few French, Americans and British added for the sake of appearances.*

A few days later, as already noted, the Japanese Government cautiously intimated to Morris its desire to undertake such an enterprise (January 17) and Balfour sounded the State Department on it (January 28). The first impulse of both House and Wilson was to oppose Japanese intervention in any form. House was convinced that it would drive Russia into the arms of Germany and, as he wrote Wilson early in March, that it would damage "that fine moral position you have given the Entente cause." He could not understand "the . . . determination of the British and French to urge the Japanese to take such a step." Implicit in House's recommendations, as in the President's notes, was the fear of the Department of State that Japan would turn the intervention into a permanent conquest of Siberia's maritime provinces. They could not well maintain their opposition on such impolitic grounds so, on House's advice, the President expressed his confidence in Japan but objected to the whole principle of intervention.

From this position the President refused to be moved by the combined importunities of the French and British. The device contrived by the latter, of an international expedition with the United States a prominent member, proved no more acceptable to him than had independent Japanese action. But circumstances were fast undermining his resolve. As the military situation in France grew more desperate in the spring of 1918 a greater measure of force attached itself to the French arguments that the eastern front must be reconstituted in some form in order to relieve the terrific German pressure on the western. From all sides, including American consular and diplomatic representatives in Russia and the Far East, came alarming reports of escaped German prisoners joining with Bolsheviks in the suppression of White efforts to renew allegiance to the Allied cause. A force of some fifty thousand Czechoslovakians, themselves liberated prisoners of war, and deserters from the Austrian army, had set out on a transcontinental journey to Vladivostok, whence they intended to return by sea to join the Allies on the western front. By June the progress of the Czechs was alleged to have been seriously impeded by Germans and Bolsheviks. Relief of the Czechs was now added to the arguments for intervention.

As General Graves, commander of the American expeditionary force in Siberia has convincingly pointed out, the Czechs never were in serious danger; German activities in that part of the world had been fantastically—or deliberately—exaggerated, and by the end of May the Allies had apparently given up any idea of sending the Czechs to the western front. The Czechs marched under orders to capture the towns they passed through, which they had little difficulty in doing. No sooner had they penetrated into eastern Siberia than they opened a widespread military campaign against the troops of the government that had permitted them to cross its territories. They remained in Siberia warring against Soviet Russia—not Germany—until finally repatriated at Allied expense in the summer of 1920—two and a half years after the reason for reconstituting the eastern front had ceased to exist, and three years after their advance guard had reached Vladivostok in safety. In one way or another the wandering Czechs served the interventionists, not excluding the United States, as a convenient pretext and a camouflage.

Because, rather than in spite of this fact, they sharpened the exigencies before which Wilson at last gave way, agreeing to the Siberian expedition July 17, 1918. He did so, however, only after it became evident that intervention would take place regardless of his permission, and probably with Japan in the leading role. He joined it not because he believed in it, or wished to join it, but because, as in the case of the consortium, he thought he could impose greater restraint on Japan within rather than outside of it. On July 17 the President in a personally drafted *aide-mémoire* to the Allied Ambassadors (which likewise became General Graves's confidential instructions), submitted his conditions. The United States was acting in deference to the wisdom of the Supreme War Council of the Allied governments. It would tolerate no interference in Russia's domestic politics. It conceived that the sole duties of the combined expeditionary forces were to assist the Czechs, help steady genuine Russian efforts at self-government and self-defense, and guard Allied military stores. It would co-operate in the discharge of these duties "with a small military force like its own from Japan, and if necessary from the other Allies" and it requested

all associated in this course of action to unite in assuring the people of Russia in the most public and solemn manner that none of the governments uniting in the action either in Siberia or in northern Russia contemplates any interference of any kind with the political sovereignty of Russia, any intervention in her internal affairs, or any impairment of her territorial integrity either now or hereafter, but that each of the associated powers has the single object of affording such aid as shall be acceptable, and only such aid as shall be acceptable, to the Russian people in their endeavor to regain control of their own affairs, their own territory, and their own destiny.

To this impressive adjuration the Allies —somewhat hypocritically, in view of the support they had already given Semenov —pledged their assent. In an exchange of notes followed by simultaneous public statements on August 3, Japan reaffirmed her "avowed policy of respecting the territorial integrity of Russia and of abstaining from all interference in her internal politics," but did not, as is commonly stated, agree to any numerical limitation of her forces. The same day a British contingent landed at Vladivostok, followed a week later by a battalion of Annamese under French command, then by the Japanese, and on August 15 and 16 two regiments of American infantry from the Philippines. The latter were joined by General Graves with additional detachments from San Francisco, September 1. The total strength of the American expeditionary force was 9,014 officers and men while Japan's ultimately exceeded 72,000.

The situation that confronted the combined forces was one that permitted each to make out of it what its leaders wished. Four White Russian war lords, Kolchak, Semenov, Kalmikov and Rozanov, held sway over different parts of Siberia. The last three were cossack gangsters who terrorized the peasantry and quarreled with each other with fine impartiality. Kolchak, an admiral in the Czar's fleet, strove for noble ends but fell a victim of his own administrative ineptitude and of circumstances beyond his control. From November, 1918, until January, 1920, he maintained a precarious rule over most of Siberia. None of the four was truly representative of the Russian people, who overthrew them all as soon as a sufficient quantity of the rifles and supplies the Allies had been furnishing Kolchak had filtered into their hands. France at first devoted what little energy she could spare the expedition to faint-hearted attempts to re-constitute the eastern front; then swung into the wake of Great Britain. Her original interest gave way to concern for the investments of French *petits rentiers* in Siberian railways which, even before the Russo-Japanese War, had been large. Great Britain seemed chiefly apprehensive of the spread of Bolshevism to India *via* China. Despite promises to the Russian people not to intervene in their domestic politics, she fought the Bolsheviks with money, arms and intrigue. Japan, on her part, was not averse to playing Semenov against Kolchak; or to fomenting by the most opportune methods at hand the disorder that she hoped would justify, or conceal, Japanese absorption of the maritime provinces.

The United States fought a long diplomatic duel with Japan, trying without success to stem the tide of Japanese reinforcements and, on the fall of Kolchak, to persuade Tokyo to withdraw its forces. Far from co-operating with the United States, Great Britain egged on the Japanese against the Bolsheviks and winked at the consequences. General Knox, the commander of the British expeditionary force, frequently caused General Graves more difficulty in observing a neutral course *vis-à-vis* the Russian civil war than did the frankly opportunistic tactics and all too obvious intrigues of Japan. By the same inter-Allied railway agreement of 1919 that had forestalled independent

Japanese control of the Chinese Eastern, the nations participating in the Siberian expedition assumed the responsibility of managing and operating the Trans-Siberian Railway in the interests of the Russian people. To the British, this meant in the interests of Kolchak. They thought that the Bolsheviks should be denied access to the road, and when General Graves refused to depart from his neutral course and take steps in this direction, they went so far as to bring pressure to bear in Washington for his removal.

Although Stevens, various consular officials and intelligence officers, and virtually the entire State Department including Lansing himself favored actively supporting Kolchak and recognizing his government, Graves held rigidly to his instructions. In his interpretation, these did not permit him to take action for or against Kolchak or his enemies save insofar as each side might benefit from the protection of the railway sectors and military stores assigned to Graves's command. Graves realized that Kolchak did not represent the wishes of the people he pretended to govern, and that his regime could not possibly survive the removal of its various foreign props. Upheld to the last by the War Department and by the President himself, the General's conduct was an object lesson in neutrality, and perhaps the only thing that prevented some kind of Franco-British deal with Japan, paying her with Russian territory for an anti-Bolshevik crusade. In any event, the American force stayed on, long after the armistice, until the complete collapse of the Kolchak regime and the diversion of Allied interest to other spheres made any such deal unlikely.

Early in January the American Government announced its intention to withdraw its troops, and pointedly intimated that it would welcome a similar move on the part of Japan. On April 1, 1920, the last American contingent sailed out of Vladivostok harbor. General Oi, the Japanese commander with whom General Graves had had many a hot altercation, "sent a band to the dock to furnish music" Graves recalls, ". . . and as the boat backed away from the dock the Japanese band began playing the good old American tune, 'Hard Times Come Again No More.' Some looked upon this tune as amusing, others as indicative of past official relations." Japan refused to withdraw her troops from Siberia until November, 1922, and she did not evacuate northern Sakhalin, seized as indemnity for losses at the hands of Soviet troops, until 1925. She had overrun northern Manchuria, and extended her privileges and influence there. She had fought pitched battles against the Bolsheviks. But she had detached no Russian territory.

The Siberian expedition was the second phase of the unfolding American offensive against Japanese expansion. In it, the United States had been forced to play a lone hand, not only receiving no co-operation from Great Britain or France, but often finding itself the dupe of Anglo-Japanese intrigue. Wilson had applied to Russia the same principles that the United States had long applied to China. Since public opinion in the United States after the war was almost hysterically anti-communistic, and since Washington would have no dealings with the Soviet, the world at large derived the impression that the chief aim of American diplomacy in the Far East was to resist Japanese aggression. This was a far cry from the policy of equal commercial opportunity that had once governed American relations with the Orient. And the war had merely paved the way for greater efforts yet to come.

II. THE CONTEMPORARY RECORD: SELECTED OFFICIAL DOCUMENTS

SECRETARY LANSING'S MEMORANDUM AND DRAFT TELEGRAM ON THE KALEDIN MOVEMENT

In early December, 1917, Secretary of State Lansing sought to clarify for himself and the President his views concerning the Bolsheviks and the possibility of aiding the Kaledin movement then developing in South Russia. On December 12, he drafted a telegram regarding the Kaledin-Kornilov movement which, with the President's "entire approval," he sent to the appropriate authorities on the following day. While both Lansing and Wilson were aware that no legal authorization existed for the direct extension of aid to an unrecognized political movement by the United States government, they sought to circumvent this problem by simply loaning the money to either the British or French who could then deliver it to Kaledin. Apparently, no direct results occurred as no actual use was made of the American authorization and no official American funds were ever actually made available to the early centers of anti-Bolshevik activity. Nevertheless, the American move represented a major decision of principle.

The Secretary of State to President Wilson

WASHINGTON, *December 10, 1917.*

MY DEAR MR. PRESIDENT: I have been considering the Russian situation and, although our information is meager and to an extent confusing, I have reached the following conclusions:

That the Bolsheviki are determined to prevent Russia from taking further part in the war.

That the longer they continue in power the more will authority in Russia be disorganized and the more will the armies disintegrate, and the harder it will become to restore order and military efficiency.

That the elimination of Russia as a fighting force will prolong the war for two or three years, with a corresponding demand upon this country for men and money.

That with Bolsheviki domination broken the Russian armies might be reorganized and become an important factor in the war by next spring or summer.

That the hope of a stable Russian Government lies for the present in a military dictatorship backed by loyal disciplined troops.

That the only apparent nucleus for an organized movement sufficiently strong to supplant the Bolsheviki and establish a government would seem to be the group of general officers with General Kaledin, the hetman of the Don Cossacks.

These conclusions present the problem

From United States Department of State, *Papers Relating to the Foreign Relations of the United States. The Lansing Papers, 1914–1920* (2 vols.; Washington, 1939–1940), II, 343–346, hereafter cited as *Lansing Papers.*

as to whether we ought to take any steps to encourage the Kaledin party, and if so the nature of those steps. . . .

Faithfully yours,

ROBERT LANSING

Draft Telegram to the Ambassador in Great Britain (Page)

The Russian situation has been carefully considered and the conclusion has been reached that the movement in the south and southeast under the leadership of Kaledine and Korniloff offers at the present time the greatest hope for the reestablishment of a stable government and the continuance of a military force on the German and Austrian fronts. While there can be no certainty of the success of Kaledine it is not improbable that he may succeed. From Moscow and Tiflis come very favorable reports as to the strength of the movement and as to the weakening power of the Bolsheviki.

In view of the policy being pursued by Lenine and Trotsky which if continued will remove Russia as a factor in the war and may even make her resources available to the Central Powers, any movement tending to prevent such a calamity should be encouraged even though its success is only a possibility.

It would seem unwise for this Government to support openly Kaledine and his party because of the attitude which it seems advisable to take with the Petrograd authorities, but it is felt that the Kaledine group should be shown that the Allied Governments are most sympathetic with his efforts. Without actually recognizing his group as a *de facto* government, which is at present impossible since it has not taken form, this Government cannot under the law loan money to him to carry forward his movement. The only practicable course seems to be for the British and French Governments to finance the Kaledine enterprise in so far as it is necessary, and for this Government to loan them the money to do so. In that way we would comply with the statute and at the same time strengthen a movement which seems to present the best possibility of retaining a Russian army in the field. . . .

PRESIDENT WILSON'S SIXTH POINT

On January 8, 1918, the President delivered his war aims address before a joint session of the two Houses of Congress. Point VI of the Fourteen Points was of special significance because of its specific reference to Russia.

VI. The evacuation of all Russian territory and such a settlement of all questions affecting Russia as will secure the best and freest cooperation of the other nations of the world in obtaining for her an unhampered and unembarrassed opportunity for the independent determination of her own political development and national policy and assure her of a sincere welcome into the society of free

From United States Department of State, *Papers Relating to the Foreign Relations of the United States, 1918. The World War* (Washington, 1933), Supplement 1, Vol. I, p. 15; hereafter cited as U.S., *Foreign Relations.*

nations under institutions of her own choosing; and, more than a welcome, assistance also of every kind that she may need and may herself desire. The treatment accorded Russia by her sister nations in the months to come will be the acid test of their good will, of their comprehension of her needs as distinguished from their own interests, and of their intelligent and unselfish sympathy.

PRESIDENT WILSON'S INITIAL RESPONSE TO LONE JAPANESE INTERVENTION

In January, 1918 the disorder in Vladivostok appeared so serious that the British and Japanese Governments dispatched war vessels to protect both property and foreign residents. About January 15, at a conference with the American Ambassador at Tokyo, the Japanese Minister of Foreign Affairs requested that if it became necessary on account of the political unrest to occupy Vladivostok and the Chinese Eastern Railway and the Amur branch, Japan be asked to do this alone. A definite request to this effect had already been sent to Great Britain. Japanese opposition to any joint military action in Siberia was emphasized by a message to the President from the Japanese Minister of Foreign Affairs delivered orally to the Counselor for the Department by an American citizen on January 24th. The minister expressed the hope that the United States would not send troops to Vladivostok or Harbin for the purpose of keeping order, as such a course would "create a very unfavorable impression in Japan." The President was much disturbed by the attitude of the Japanese Government. His response to both these requests is indicated in the notes that follow.

*President Wilson to the
Secretary of State*

WASHINGTON, *20 January, 1918.*

MY DEAR MR. SECRETARY: The suggestion made by the Japanese government in this despatch seems to me very significant of possible coming events, and I would be very much obliged to you if you would tell me what reply you think should be made to it.

The fact that the Japanese are sending a larger naval force to Vladivostok than they at first led us to expect makes an uncomfortable impression on me, particularly in view of this latest request.

It seems to me clear that we should show very clearly in our reply that we should look upon military action in that quarter with distinct disapproval.

Faithfully yours,

W. W.

*President Wilson to the Counselor for
the Department of State (Polk)*

WASHINGTON, *28 January, 1918.*

MY DEAR MR. COUNSELOR: Thank you for the enclosed. I dare say that for the present we may let this matter stand as it does but I hope that we shall soon have new material for judgment in the shape of further information from our Ambassador at Tokyo. I do not think that it will be safe or wise to leave the Japanese government in any doubt as to the impression such an attitude on their part makes on us.

Faithfully Yours,

W. W.

PRESIDENT WILSON ON THE ALLIED REQUEST FOR JAPANESE INTERVENTION

On February 27, 1918, the British and French ambassadors to the United States requested President Wilson's solution to the problem of military intervention in Siberia. Japan should either be requested to intervene by the allies or be allowed to proceed independently. It seemed to be an accepted fact that Japan would send troops to Vladivostok and Harbin. In these circumstances, the President decided that it was useless to oppose intervention by Japan. He sent a note to the Secretary of State on March 1 in which he stated that he had no objection to a request being made by the Allied governments that Japan act in Siberia but that for certain reasons the United States would not join them in making such a request. The telegram below was shown to the British, French, and Italian ambassadors, but was not sent.

The Government of the United States is made constantly aware at every turn of events that it is the desire of the people of the United States that, while cooperating with all its energy with its associates in the war in every direct enterprise of the war in which it is possible for it to take part, it should leave itself diplomatically free wherever it can do so without injustice to its associates. It is for this reason that the Government of the United States has not thought it wise to join the governments of the Entente in asking the Japanese government to act in Siberia. It has no objection to that request being made, and it wishes to assure the Japanese government that it has entire confidence that in putting an armed force into Siberia it is doing so as an ally of Russia, with no purpose but to save Siberia from the invasion of the armies and intrigues of Germany and with entire willingness to leave the determination of all questions that may affect the permanent fortunes of Siberia to the Council of Peace.

Lansing Papers, II, p. 355.

DECLARATION OF THE U. S. GOVERNMENT AGAINST
INTERVENTION, MARCH 5, 1918

At the President's request the draft statement quoted above was not given to the Japanese chargé when he called at the State Department on March 2. As a result of messages received from Colonel Edward M. House and William C. Bullitt emphasizing the moral position of the United States and concern over independent Japanese action, the President changed his mind and reverted to his earlier stand on intervention. This stand was reflected in the message below from the Acting Secretary of State to Ambassador Morris in Japan.

WASHINGTON, *March 5, 1918, 4 p.m.*

At your earliest opportunity you will please read to the Japanese Government the following message but leave no copy unless they request you to do so:

The Government of the United States has been giving the most careful and anxious consideration to the conditions now prevailing in Siberia and their possible remedy. It realizes the extreme danger of anarchy to which the Siberian provinces are exposed and the imminent risk also of German invasion and domination. It shares with the governments of the Entente the view that, if intervention is deemed wise, the Government of Japan is in the best situation to undertake it and could accomplish it most efficiently. It has, moreover, the utmost confidence in the Japanese Government and would be entirely willing, so far as its own feelings towards that Government are concerned, to intrust the enterprise to it. But it is bound in frankness to say that the wisdom of intervention seems to it most questionable. If it were undertaken the Government of the United States assumes that the most explicit assurance would be given that it was undertaken by Japan as an ally of Russia, in Russia's interest, and with the sole view of holding it safe against Germany and at the absolute disposal of the final peace conference. Otherwise the Central powers could and would make it appear that Japan was doing in the East exactly what Germany is doing in the West and so seek to counter the condemnation which all the world must pronounce against Germany's invasion of Russia, which she attempts to justify on the pretext of restoring order. And it is the judgment of the Government of the United States, uttered with the utmost respect, that, even with such assurances given, they could in the same way be discredited by those whose interest it was to discredit them; that a hot resentment would be generated in Russia itself, and that the whole action might play into the hands of the enemies of Russia, and particularly of the enemies of the Russian revolution, for which the Government of the United States entertains the greatest sympathy, in spite of all the unhappiness and misfortune which has for the time being sprung out of it. The Government of the United States begs once more to express to the Government of Japan its warmest friendship and confidence and once more begs it to accept these expressions of judgment as uttered only in the frankness of friendship.

POLK

U.S., *Foreign Relations, Russia, 1918* (3 vols.; Washington, 1931–1932), II, pp. 67–68.

WILSON CONTINUES TO OPPOSE INTERVENTION

Throughout the month of March, President Wilson received appeals from his allies as well as from the Supreme War Council, urging his consent to Japanese intervention as a mandatory of the Allies. At one point when he received a stack of memoranda on the Siberian question, he wrote Lansing, "I must say that none of these memoranda has anything in it that is at all persuasive to me. I hope that you feel the same way." The note below to the Secretary of State indicates the misgivings that remained in Wilson's mind concerning Japanese intervention.

WASHINGTON, 22 *March, 1918*
MY DEAR MR. SECRETARY: I am much obliged to you for sending these papers to me so promptly, but I do not find them sufficient cause for altering our position. They still do not answer the question I have put to Lord Reading and to all oth-

ers who argue in favour of intervention by Japan, namely, What is it to effect and how will it be efficacious in effecting it? The condition of Siberia furnishes no answer.

Faithfully Yours,

W. W.

Lansing Papers, II, p. 357.

SECRETARY LANSING REVIEWS THE PRISONER OF WAR MENACE

At the end of March, 1918, Secretary Lansing wrote the President revealing the chaotic state of affairs in Siberia and expressing his views on lone Japanese military action as a mandatory of the Allies in Siberia. The President responded orally that he was not prepared to change the policy adopted which was against military intervention. Lansing's summary of the Siberian situation appears below.

WASHINGTON, *March 24, 1918.*
MY DEAR MR. PRESIDENT: If the reports, which persist, that the military prisoners in Siberia are being organized under German officers and have succeeded in occupying Irkutsk are confirmed, we will have a new situation in Siberia which may cause a revision of our policy. It would seem to me, therefore, that we should consider the problem on the hypothesis that the reports are true and be prepared to act with promptness.

The occupation of important points in eastern Siberia by a German military force and the helpless state of the Russians to resist the extension of the German power place the situation on an entirely different basis from the one presented by the chaotic state caused by quarreling Russian factions. The presence of the Germans and the possibility of their control of Siberia becomes a real menace to the peace of the Far East. The situation of Irkutsk is such that the Ger-

Lansing Papers, II, pp. 357–358.

mans, if masters of the place, might invade Manchuria and obtain control of the Trans-Siberian Railway.

In view of these facts I do not see how Japan could be expected to refrain from taking military measures to resist further extension of the German power, nor do I think that we could reasonably oppose their resistance to the German advance in that region. In fact I believe that in the circumstances Japan will act whether we approve or not. Would it then be the better policy to approve or to be in opposition to Japanese intervention?

With the actual control by the Germans of so important a place as Irkutsk the question of the moral effect upon the Russian people of an expedition against the Germans is a very different thing from the occupation of the Siberian Railway in order to keep order between contending Russian factions. It would seem to be a legitimate operation against the common enemy. I do not see how we could refuse to sanction such a military step.

The question presented, if intervention in Siberia seems advisable, is whether Japan alone or the Powers arrayed against Germany acting jointly should constitute the expeditionary force employed to overthrow the German power. I think that we must concede that in any event the burden of this task must fall upon Japan. No Power has forces available for this undertaking sufficiently strong to be a real factor in achieving the end desired. Furthermore Japan seems to be opposed to joint action. In the circumstances are not Japan's sensibilities more important than the sensibilities of the Russian people?

If the reports turn out to be correct will we lose anything by making Japan the mandatory of the Powers, and giving approval to her sending an expeditionary force into Siberia to oust the Germans and to restore Russian authority in that region?

Ought we not to adopt this policy in the event that Irkutsk is actually controlled by the Germans?

I think that the situation requires careful consideration and a policy should be adopted in advance because no time ought to be lost to meet and offset the German activities in Siberia, if the reports prove to be correct.

Faithfully yours,

ROBERT LANSING

SUBSTANCE OF THE SINO-JAPANESE NOTE, MARCH 25, 1918

The State Department had been aware since February 23, 1918, that negotiations for a Sino-Japanese Military agreement had been in progress. Yet the Department had found it difficult to protest against the measure since it was ostensibly aimed at a common foe. The following note was handed to the Secretary of State by the Japanese Ambassador, May 18, 1918.

The German influence steadily penetrating into the Russian territories and threatening the general peace and security in the Far East, the two Governments will consider in common what measure should be taken in order to meet the situation and to do their part in the allied cause.

The co-operation between the two armed forces in the joint defensive movements against the enemy will be arranged by the competent Authorities of the two Governments who will from time to time consult freely upon all questions of mutual interest. The Arrangement reached by said competent Authorities will be put into operation only at such time as the two governments may eventually decide.

MINISTER PAUL S. REINSCH AND PRESIDENT WILSON ON THE CZECHOSLOVAK CONFLICT IN SIBERIA

Throughout April and May appeals for intervention in Siberia increased. While Japan had evidently ceased to object to cooperative action in Siberia, the President had not approved uniting with Allied governments in requesting Japan to engage in an inter-Allied expedition. In the early part of June reports arrived that the Czechoslovak forces in western Siberia were trying to make their way to Vladivostok. Later, about June 20, came the report that the Bolsheviks were opposing this movement and that the refugees had been compelled to fight the Red Guards along the Siberian Railway. On June 13 the minister in China, Paul S. Reinsch, presented his view of the Czechoslovak incident. President Wilson's response to this note is significant. Below is the note sent by Reinsch and the response of the President.

The Minister in China (Reinsch) to the Secretary of State

PEKING, *June 13, 1918, 5 p.m.*

It is the general opinion of Allied representatives here in which I concur that it would be a serious mistake to remove the Czecho-Slovak troops from Siberia. With only slight countenance and support they could control all of Siberia against the Germans. They are sympathetic to the Russian population, eager to be accessories to the Allied cause, the most serious means [menace] to extension of German influence in Russia. Their removal would greatly benefit Germany and further discourage Russia. If they

U.S., *Foreign Relations, 1918, Russia,* II, pp. 206–207.

were not in Siberia it would be worth while to bring them there from a distance.

Representatives of the Moscow Central Supply Committee here at present describe the nature of their organization, elective in its communal, district and central bodies, devoted to task of filling crying needs Russian population, saving lives, resisting extension of German influence, preventing supplies to regions under German control. They seem an organization which Allies could support with good results. They are working here for relaxation of Manchurian export embargo. Do you desire that I support release of merchandise addressed to that committee?

REINSCH

President Wilson to the Secretary of State

WASHINGTON, *17 June, 1918.*

MY DEAR MR. SECRETARY: There seems to me to emerge from this suggestion the

shadow of a plan that might be worked, with Japanese and other assistance. These people are the cousins of the Russians.

Faithfully Yours,

W. W.

Lansing Papers, II, p. 363.

SECRETARY LANSING ON THE CZECHOSLOVAK CONFLICT

On June 23, Secretary Lansing wrote the President that the Czech incident seemed to him to have created a new condition in the problem of intervention in Siberia, and that means of aiding the Czechs should be considered.

WASHINGTON, *June 23, 1918.*

MY DEAR MR. PRESIDENT:

The situation of the Czecho-Slovak forces in western Siberia seems to me to create a new condition which should receive careful consideration. Prof. Masaryk assured me that these rebels against Austria-Hungary, collected from the Russian prison camps and from deserters, would not fight against the Russians but only sought to pass via Vladivostok to the western front.

Now it appears that their efforts to reach Vladivostok being opposed by the Bolsheviks they are fighting the Red Guards along the Siberian line with more or less success. As these troops are most

loyal to our cause and have been most unjustly treated by the various Soviets ought we not to consider whether something cannot be done to support them?

There are, it seems, between 10,000 and 15,000 at Vladivostok and some 40,-000 to 60,000 in western Siberia. In the latter territory Omsk and Tomsk are reported to be in their hands. Is it not possible that in this body of capable and loyal troops may be found a nucleus for military occupation of the Siberian railway?

I would like to confer with you on the subject after cabinet-meeting Tuesday if you find it convenient.

Faithfully yours,

ROBERT LANSING

Lansing Papers, II, p. 364.

JAPANESE REPLY TO THE ALLIED GOVERNMENTS ON COMMON ACTION IN SIBERIA

On June 26, Viscount Ishii, the Japanese Ambassador, read to the Secretary of State a cablegram from his government, and later sent a paraphrase of it which follows.

Lansing Papers, II, p. 365.

As the result of the Versailles Conference, His Britannic Majesty's Principal Secretary of State for Foreign Affairs, in the name of the Governments of Great Britain, France and Italy, had recently proposed to the Imperial Government to consent to undertake certain common action in Siberia, subject to the concurrence of the American Government. The Imperial Government still hold the same view as expressed to the American Government on the 19th March last and attach great importance to the positive support of the latter in considering any action of intervention in Siberia. Accordingly, a reply has been sent in the sense that the Japanese Government, while deeply appreciating the proposal, could not feel at liberty to express their decision before a complete and satisfactory understanding on the question was reached between the three Powers and the United States.

RECOMMENDATIONS OF LT. COL. RAYMOND ROBINS ON THE RUSSIAN SITUATION

Secretary Lansing sent the following telegram, which he had received from Lieutenant Colonel Raymond Robins, to the President. The President responded as follows on July 3: "Thank you for having let me see the enclosed. . . . I differ from them only in practical details. Cordially and faithfully yours, Woodrow Wilson." Robins' recommendations appear below.

WASHINGTON, *July 1, 1918.*

SIR: Pursuant to your request I have the honor to present to you herewith a brief printed statement of my recommendations concerning the Russian situation.

It seems to me that in all the confusion of statement and conclusion surrounding the Russian situation the following propositions are reasonably clear:

First, that Germany hesitates to employ in Russia armed forces in sufficient number to subjugate the land but desires—as clearly indicated by a consistent course of conduct in Ukrainia, Finland and the Baltic Provinces—to establish so-called governments of law and order which are too weak to support themselves in the great class struggle but which may be maintained and controlled by German force.

Second, that through such governments Germany hopes to control and utilize Russian resources and, if possible, Russian man-power against the Western Allies in this war, and to conclude the war with Russia completely under the economic dominion of Germany.

Third, that forcible Allied intervention opposed by the Soviets would be essentially analogous to what Germany is doing in the Ukraine, in Finland and in the Baltic Provinces.

Fourth, that such intervention unless welcomed by the great mass of the Russian people would be destructive in principle of the entire basis of President Wilson's democratic war policy.

Lansing Papers, II, pp. 365–366.

Fifth, that forcible Allied intervention, if uninvited by the Soviet power, will certainly be opposed and will result in civil war.

Sixth, that forcible Allied intervention can not be justified upon grounds of military necessity, and will not prevent but will hasten and make easy the consummation of Germany's war aims in European Russia.

Seventh, that American economic co-operation with Russia will open the way for effective Allied intervention with force and the creation of an actual fighting front opposed to Germany in Russia.

The recommendations enclosed herewith are stated with as much brevity as possible.

Respectfully,

RAYMOND ROBINS

SUPREME WAR COUNCIL'S APPEAL TO PRESIDENT WILSON TO SUPPORT ALLIED INTERVENTION, JULY 2, 1918

Unable to take action on the Japanese expedition without American consent, the Supreme War Council prepared and sent to the Secretary of State a comprehensive memorandum designed to gain the support of President Wilson. A portion of the message appears below.

PARIS, *July 2, 1918, midnight, and*

July 3, 1 a.m.

... For these reasons the Supreme War Council, having carefully considered the military situation and the prospects of the Allies in all the theaters of war, have come to conclusion —

I. That immediate Allied armed assistance to Russia is imperatively necessary for the following reasons:

(*a*) To assist the Russian nation to throw off their German oppressors and to prevent the unlimited military and economic domination of Russia by Germany in her own interests.

(*b*) For the decisive military reason given by General Foch in his telegram to President Wilson; i.e., that the Germans have already called back from Russia a number of divisions and sent them to the western front. Allied intervention will be the first step in stimulating the national uprising in Russia against German domination which will have an immediate effect in renewing German anxiety in regard to the east and compelling her to refrain from removing further troops westward and perhaps to move troops back to the east.

(*c*) To shorten the war by the reconstitution of the Russian front.

(*d*) To prevent the isolation of Russia from western Europe. They are advised that if action is not taken in Siberia the existing Allied forces in northern Russia may have to be withdrawn and Russia will be completely cut off from the Allies.

(*e*) To deny to Germany the supplies of western Siberia and the important military stores at Vladivostok and

U.S., *Foreign Relations, 1918, Russia*, II, pp. 245–246.

to render these available for the Russian population.

(f) To bring assistance to the Czecho-Slovak forces which have made great sacrifices to the cause for which we are fighting.

II. That the intervention should be Allied in character, should be accompanied by pledges to the Russian people as agreed to at the last Versailles conference, and should include the following:

1. An Allied force to operate in Siberia. Circumstances render imperative that the force shall be considerable in number, military in character and Allied in composition, and that above all things it should operate immediately; delay would be fatal. It is recognized that owing to geographical and shipping conditions Japanese troops will comprise the larger portion of the force but its Allied character must be maintained and it must include American and Allied units. The force should be under a single command appointed by the power that provides the largest number of troops.

2. Such developments of the Allied forces in Murmansk and Archangel as the military advisers of the Allies may recommend.

3. Relief expeditions under American direction and control to supply the wants and alleviate the sufferings of the Russian people.

The primary object of Allied action being to cooperate with the Russian nation in re-creating the eastern front as a first step towards freeing Russia, the closest coordination must exist between the above forces and the Russian people.

III. Therefore, in view of —

1. The unanimous opinion of General Foch and the Allied military advisers of the Supreme War Council that immediate dispatch of a considerable Allied force to Siberia is essential for the victory of the Allied armies;

2. The fact that no adequate expedition can be sent without Japanese cooperation and that Japan will not undertake effective action without the encouragement and support of the United States Government; and

3. The shortness of the time available before the winter for initiating active operations in Siberia and the rapid German penetration into Russia:

the Supreme War Council appeal to President Wilson to approve the policy here recommended and thus to enable it to be carried into effect before it is too late.

FRAZIER

SECRETARY LANSING'S MEMORANDUM OF A CONFERENCE
ON THE SIBERIAN SITUATION

A conference was held at the White House on July 6 in regard to the Siberian situation. Here the President announced his intention to support a limited intervention in Siberia.

Present: The President, the Secretary of State, the Secretary of War, the Secretary of the Navy, General March, and Admiral Benson.

After debating the whole subject of the present conditions in Siberia as affected by the taking of Vladivostok by the Czecho-Slovaks, the landing of American, British, French, and Japanese forces from the naval vessels in that port, and the occupation of the railroad through western Siberia by other Czecho-Slovaks with the reported taking of Irkutsk by these troops; and after reading and discussing the communication of the Supreme War Council favoring an attempt to restore an eastern front against the Central powers; and also a memorandum by the Secretary of State —

The following propositions and program were decided upon:

(1) That the establishment of an eastern front through a military expedition, even if it was wise to employ a large Japanese force, is physically impossible though the front was established east of the Ural Mountains;

(2) That under present conditions any advance westward of Irkutsk does not seem possible and needs no further consideration;

(3) That the present situation of the Czecho-Slovaks requires this Government and other governments to make an effort to aid those at Vladivostok in forming a junction with their compatriots in western Siberia; and that this Government on sentimental grounds and because of the effect upon the friendly Slavs everywhere would be subject to criticism if it did not make this effort and would doubtless be held responsible if they were defeated by lack of such effort;

(4) That in view of the inability of the United States to furnish any considerable force within a short time to assist the Czecho-Slovaks the following plan of operations should be adopted, provided the Japanese Government agrees to cooperate;

(a) The furnishing of small arms, machine guns, and ammunition to the Czecho-Slovaks at Vladivostok by the Japanese Government; this Government to share expense and to supplement the supplies as rapidly as possible;

(b) The assembling of a military force at Vladivostok composed of approximately 7,000 Americans and 7,000 Japanese to guard the line of communication of the Czecho-Slovaks proceeding toward Irkutsk; the Japanese to send troops at once;

(c) The landing of available forces from the American and Allied naval vessels to hold possession of Vladivostok and cooperate with the Czecho-Slovaks;

U.S., *Foreign Relations, 1918, Russia*, II, pp. 262–263.

(d) The public announcement by this and Japanese Governments that the purpose of landing troops is to aid Czecho-Slovaks against German and Austrian prisoners, that there is no purpose to interfere with internal affairs of Russia, and that they guarantee not to impair the political or territorial sovereignty of Russia; and

(e) To await further developments before taking further steps.

[File copy not signed]

AMERICAN PROPOSALS FOR MILITARY ACTION, JULY 17, 1918

In mid-July, the Secretary of State presented to the Allied Ambassadors an aide-mémoire *concerning military action in Russia. The statement had been drafted by the President himself.*

The whole heart of the people of the United States is in the winning of this war. The controlling purpose of the Government of the United States is to do everything that is necessary and effective to win it. It wishes to cooperate in every practicable way with the Allied Governments, and to cooperate ungrudgingly; for it has no ends of its own to serve and believes that the war can be won only by common counsel and intimate concert of action. It has sought to study every proposed policy or action in which its cooperation has been asked in this spirit, and states the following conclusions in the confidence that, if it finds itself obliged to decline participation in any undertaking or course of action, it will be understood that it does so only because it deems itself precluded from participating by imperative considerations either of policy or of fact.

In full agreement with the Allied Governments and upon the unanimous advice of the Supreme War Council, the Government of the United States adopted, upon its entrance into the war, a plan for taking part in the fighting on the western front into which all its resources of men and material were to be put, and put as rapidly as possible, and it has carried out that plan with energy and success, pressing its execution more and more rapidly forward and literally putting into it the entire energy and executive force of the nation. This was its response, its very willing and hearty response, to what was the unhesitating judgment alike of its own military advisers and of the advisers of the Allied Governments. It is now considering, at the suggestion of the Supreme War Council, the possibility of making very considerable additions even to this immense program which, if they should prove feasible at all, will tax the industrial processes of the United States and the shipping facilities of the whole group of associated nations to the utmost. It has thus concentrated all its plans and all its resources upon this single absolutely necessary object.

In such circumstances it feels it to be its duty to say that it cannot, so long as the military situation on the western front remains critical, consent to break or slacken the force of its present effort by diverting any part of its military force to other points or objectives. The United States is at a great distance from the field of action on the western front; it is at a much greater distance from any other field of action. The instrumentalities by which it is to handle its armies and its stores have at great cost and with great difficulty been created in France. They do not exist elsewhere. It is practicable for her to do a great deal in France; it is not practicable for her to do anything of importance or on a large scale upon any other field. The American Government, therefore, very respectfully requests its associates to accept its deliberate judgment that it should not dissipate its force by attempting important operations elsewhere.

It regards the Italian front as closely coordinated with the western front, however, and is willing to divert a portion of its military forces from France to Italy if it is the judgment and wish of the Supreme Command that it should do so. It wishes to defer to the decision of the Commander in Chief in this matter, as it would wish to defer in all others, particularly because it considers these two fronts so closely related as to be practically but separate parts of a single line and because it would be necessary that any American troops sent to Italy should be subtracted from the number used in France and be actually transported across French territory from the ports now used by the armies of the United States.

It is the clear and fixed judgment of the Government of the United States, arrived at after repeated and very searching reconsiderations of the whole situation in Russia, that military intervention there would add to the present sad confusion in Russia rather than cure it, injure her rather than help her, and that it would be of no advantage in the prosecution of our main design, to win the war against Germany. It can not, therefore, take part in such intervention or sanction it in principle. Military intervention would, in its judgment, even supposing it to be efficacious in its immediate avowed object of delivering an attack upon Germany from the east, be merely a method of making use of Russia, not a method of serving her. Her people could not profit by it, if they profited by it at all, in time to save them from their present distresses, and their substance would be used to maintain foreign armies, not to reconstitute their own. Military action is admissible in Russia, as the Government of the United States sees the circumstances, only to help the Czecho-Slovaks consolidate their forces and get into successful cooperation with their Slavic kinsmen and to steady any efforts at self-government or self-defense in which the Russians themselves may be willing to accept assistance. Whether from Vladivostok or from Murmansk and Archangel, the only legitimate object for which American or Allied troops can be employed, it submits, is to guard military stores which may subsequently be needed by Russian forces and to render such aid as may be acceptable to the Russians in the organization of their own self-defense. For helping the Czecho-Slovaks there is immediate necessity and sufficient justification. Recent developments have made it evident that that is in the interest of what the Russian people themselves desire, and the Government of the United States is glad to contribute the small force at its disposal for that purpose. It yields, also, to the judgment of the Supreme Command in the matter of establishing a small force at Murmansk, to guard the military stores at Kola, and to make it safe for Russian forces to come together in organized bodies in the north. But it owes it to frank counsel to say that it can go no further than these modest and experimental plans. It is not in a position, and has no expectation of being in a position, to take part in organized intervention in adequate force from either Vladivostok or Murmansk and Archangel. It feels that it ought to add, also, that it will feel at liberty to use the few troops it can spare only for the purposes here stated and shall feel obliged to withdraw those forces, in order to add them to the forces at the western front, if the plans in whose execution it is now intended that they should cooperate should develop into others inconsistent with the policy to which the Government of the United States feels constrained to restrict itself.

At the same time the Government of the United States wishes to say with the utmost cordiality and good will that none of the conclusions here stated is meant to wear the least color of criticism of what the other governments associated against Germany may think it wise to undertake. It wishes in no way to embarrass their choices of policy. All that is intended here is a perfectly frank and definite statement of the policy which the United States feels obliged to adopt for herself and in the use of her own military forces. The Government of the United States does not wish it to be understood that in so restricting its own activities it is seeking, even by implication, to set limits to the action or to define the policies of its associates.

It hopes to carry out the plans for safeguarding the rear of the Czecho-Slovaks operating from Vladivostok in a way that will place it and keep it in close cooperation with a small military force like its own from Japan, and if necessary from the other Allies, and that will assure it of the cordial accord of all the Allied powers; and it proposes to ask all associated in this course of action to unite in assuring the people of Russia in the most public and solemn manner that none of the governments uniting in action either in Siberia or in northern Russia contemplates any interference of any kind with the political sovereignty of Russia, any intervention in her internal affairs, or any impairment of her territorial integrity either now or hereafter, but that each of the associated powers has the single object of affording such aid as shall be acceptable, and only such aid as shall be acceptable, to the Russian people in their endeavor to regain control of their own affairs, their own territory, and their own destiny.

It is the hope and purpose of the Government of the United States to take advantage of the earliest opportunity to send to Siberia a commission of merchants, agricultural experts, labor advisers, Red Cross representatives, and agents of the Young Men's Christian Association accustomed to organizing the best methods of spreading useful information and rendering educational help of a modest sort, in order in some systematic manner to relieve the immediate economic necessities of the people there in every way for which opportunity may open. The execution of this plan will follow and will not be permitted to embarrass the military assistance rendered in the rear of the westward-moving forces of the Czecho-Slovaks.

WASHINGTON, *July 17, 1918.*

THE U. S. OPPOSES UNIFIED POLITICAL DIRECTION OF
INTERVENTION AND INCREASE OF FORCES

*No sooner had American troops arrived in Siberia than the Allies
sought to extend the scope and nature of the mission. The following
notes indicate the United States Government's response to these efforts.*

*Memorandum of the Secretary of State
on Siberian Policy after Conference with
the President, August 20, 1918*[1]

This Government can not aid in equipping, transporting or maintaining any troops beyond the numbers agreed upon between the United States and Japan.

This Government is not in favor of proceeding west of Irkutsk in relieving the Czecho-Slovaks in western Siberia.

This Government favors the retirement of Czecho-Slovaks eastward from western Siberia as rapidly as safety will permit and the concentration of all troops in eastern Siberia where they should jointly operate against the hostile forces along the Amur River and about Lake Baikal.

This Government prefers to defer a consideration of the future movements of the Czecho-Slovaks whether eastward to France or westward to Russia until after eastern Siberia has been cleared of enemies.

*The Secretary of State to
President Wilson*[2]

WASHINGTON, *August 22, 1918.*

MY DEAR MR. PRESIDENT: I lay before you a communication from the French Embassy in relation to the sending of High Commissioners to Siberia — and also a memorandum from Mr. Phillips on the subject.

Personally I feel that in view of our policy it would be unwise to do this and that this is another move to impress our action in Siberia with the character of intervention rather than relief of the Czechs. The suggestion that our High Commissioner be the head of an international commission seems to be a bait to draw us into this policy which has been so insistently urged by Great Britain for the past six months.

It would relieve the situation if you authorized me to say to the Ambassadors that we did not intend to appoint a High Commissioner and to state to the press that at present we had no intention of making such an appointment.

If we decline to cooperate in this I believe that the Commission will have little weight.

Faithfully yours,

ROBERT LANSING

President Wilson to the Secretary of State[2]

WASHINGTON, *23 August, 1918.*

MY DEAR MR. SECRETARY: I hope you will do just what you here suggest. The other governments are going much further than we and much faster, — are, indeed, acting upon a plan which is altogether foreign from ours and inconsistent with it.

Please make it plain to the French Ambassador that we do not think cooperation in political action necessary or desirable in eastern Siberia because we

[1] U.S., *Foreign Relations, 1918, Russia*, II, p. 351.
[2] *Lansing Papers*, II, pp. 378–379.

contemplate no political action of any kind there, but only the action of friends who stand at hand and wait to see how they can help. The more plain and emphatic this is made the less danger will there be or [of?] subsequent misunderstandings and irritations.

Faithfully Yours,

W. W.

The Secretary of State to the French Ambassador (Jusserand)[3]

No. 2220

WASHINGTON, *August 31, 1918*

EXCELLENCY: I have the honor to acknowledge the receipt of your excellency's note of August 12, 1918, in regard to the coordination of the action of the Allies in Siberia and northern Russia. You advise me that your Government believes that it would be wise to organize an inter-Allied civilian board charged, among other duties, with that of safeguarding unity of action towards the Russian people, of deciding political disputes and of defining the attitude between the Allied Governments and local authorities; and you are good enough to suggest that the chairmanship of such a board would go to a representative from the United States.

In this connection I beg to inform you that the Government of the United States feels confident that, upon their arrival, cordial cooperation will govern the relations between the representatives of the United States and the representatives of the Allied nations, but believes that the means by which such essential *liaison* may best be effected must await the arrival in Siberia of the respective officials. The foregoing refers to the cooperation in such relief as it may be decided to extend in eastern Siberia, as distinct from any political activities which governments may choose to exercise there. Moreover, as has been publicly announced in the press of this country, it is the hope and expectation of the Government of the United States that the governments with which it is associated will lend their active aid in the execution of these plans.

Since the beginning of the revolutionary movement this Government has maintained an attitude of strict impartiality as between contending political parties and, as it contemplates no change in this attitude, it deems cooperation in any political action impossible and believes it would be as unnecessary as it is undesirable. It prefers to occupy a position in eastern Siberia merely as a friend who stands at hand ready to help in the most practical and wholehearted manner.

While, therefore, this Government cannot see its way clear to concur in the suggestion that a representative of the United States should assume the chairmanship of such an inter-Allied board, I beg to express my appreciation of your excellency's courtesy and consideration.

Furthermore, I improve this opportunity to inform your excellency that, while the matter of the extension of economic relief to the Siberian people is receiving constant and attentive consideration, this Government has not as yet definitely determined upon the action it will take in that respect.

Accept [etc.] ROBERT LANSING

---

[3] U.S., *Foreign Relations, 1918, Russia*, II, p. 362.

THE U. S. GOVERNMENT OPPOSES THE SIZE AND ACTIONS OF JAPANESE FORCES IN SIBERIA AND MANCHURIA

On November 16, 1918, five days after the armistice in Europe had removed one of the major rationales for Allied intervention in Russia, Secretary Lansing made the first of numerous representations through Ambassador Morris to Tokyo concerning Japanese actions in Siberia and North Manchuria. The United States protested against the number of Japanese troops in eastern Asia, which by this time totaled something around 72,400, as well as the monopoly of control which they exercised there. The note stressed the need of placing John F. Stevens and the Russian Railway Service Corps in charge of operating the Siberian railways in behalf of Russia.

WASHINGTON, *November 16, 1918, noon.*

. . . Please take up frankly with the Japanese Government the following points:

1. The United States has viewed with surprise the presence of the very large number of Japanese troops now in north Manchuria and eastern Siberia. Reliable information shows the number of these troops to be so great as to constitute a definite departure from the express understanding for cooperation between Japan and the United States and quite unwarranted by any military necessity.

2. This Government believes that any undertaking in regard to the Siberian situation must be based on a spirit of frank and open cooperation. It is convinced that any monopoly of control such as that now exercised by Japan in north Manchuria and in the eastern part of the Trans-Baikal will arouse suspicion and prove open to the charges of exploitation. Such monopoly is certainly opposed not only to the purpose of this Government to assist Russia but also to its views regarding China.

3. In suggesting that Mr. Stevens assume charge of railway operations, as representing Russia and not the United States or any interest of the United States, this Government had the express intention not to modify any previously existing rights of Russia or China. The memorandum of agreement, approved by all the Allied representatives at Vladivostok and by Russian authorities, expressly provides for supervision by international or Russian control and not by any one power. In other words, every measure advocated by this Government has had the purpose of avoiding a monopoly of control creating conditions such as would arouse alarm or suspicion. Moreover, in the opinion of this Government, the question of railway operation is a practical one which the welfare of the Russian people requires should be met by practical measures. Such practical measures of assistance had already been undertaken by the United States, acting in behalf of Russia, in 1917 when Mr. Stevens was requested by the Russian railway administration to secure the assistance of the Russian Railway Service Corps. Furthermore this Government is convinced that a divided control of the operation of the Siberian railway system is foredoomed to failure.

U.S., *Foreign Relations, 1918, Russia,* II, pp. 433–435.

4. The Government of the United States believes that fundamentally the Government of Japan shares its views and that the United States and Japan have a common purpose in the part each has played in the present war, in full accord with the Governments associated against the military autocracies of the Central powers. Each is mutually concerned that the peoples with whom it comes in contact shall be safeguarded from aggression. It was in this spirit of confidence that the Government of the United States approached the Japanese Government in regard to joint action of assistance in Siberia. This Government therefore deems it only the part of frankness and friendly counsel to point out how far in practice the military undertakings of Japan appear now to have diverged from the previously declared purpose of the two Governments.

I am presenting these same points to the Japanese Ambassador here to-day. Please let me know at the earliest opportunity the result of such action as you may be able to take at Tokyo. At the same time, let me have your views (1) as to the advisability of sending along the railway as far as Omsk such American troops as may now be available; (2) in the event Japan declines to alter its present policy, what would be the effect of withdrawing from Siberia all American forces, including Stevens and the Russian Railway Service Corps, as evidence of our unwillingness to be associated with a policy so contrary to our declared purpose regarding Russia. The possibility of such action was expressly declared in the *aide-mémoire* handed to the Japanese Ambassador at Washington under date of July 17.

Repeat to Peking for its information.

LANSING

PRESIDENT WILSON APPROVES A BRIEFING ON THE SIBERIAN SITUATION

By January 1919, American public opinion was becoming extremely restive on the whole subject of Russia. In the meantime, however, the American government had succeeded in negotiating a railway plan which required that American troops remain in Siberia to support Stevens, the head of the railway mission, and guard the railway. The execution of the railway plan required funds as well as troops. Thus it was necessary to seek additional money from Congress or else appropriate it from the President's private fund. In view of this problem, the President's advice was sought. After careful consideration with Secretary Lansing of the cables describing the Siberian situation, the President, then in France at the peace conference, approved and authorized the Acting Secretary of State to follow the procedure quoted below.

U.S., *Foreign Relations, 1919, Russia* (Washington, 1937), pp. 246–248.

Paris, *January 31, 1919, 8 p.m.*

. . . You are requested to ask for a second [*secret*] hearing before such committee or committees in Congress as you think best. At this hearing you will state that it is the President's wish that the Siberian situation and the activities of the administration in relation thereto be made known fully and frankly, though in strict confidence, to the members of these committees. You will then develop the strategic importance both from the point of view of Russia and of the United States of the Trans-Siberian Railway as being a principal means of access to and from the Russian people and as affording an opportunity for economic aid to Siberia where the people are relatively friendly and resistant to Bolshevik influence and where there are large bodies of Czech-Slovaks who rely upon our support as well as large numbers of enemy prisoners of war whose activities must be watched and in all cases [*if necessary*] controlled. The potential value of this railroad as a means for developing American commerce particularly from the west coast of the United States to Russia might be mentioned. You may then narrate in considerable detail the difficulties which we have had with Japan with reference to this railway and in particular the action of Japan in practically seizing the Chinese Eastern Railway, thereby in effect controlling all intercourse to and from Russia via the Pacific. You might mention the number of troops sent by Japan for the purpose and point out that such number was far in excess of that contemplated by the arrangement under which troops of the Associated Governments were landed in Siberia. The nature of the activities of Japan including disposition of their troops and Japanese commercial activities should then be referred to [followed by] a statement of the efforts of the Government of the United States to restore the railroad to a condition where it would not be exclusively dominated by any one power. . . . The conversations of the President and Secretary of State with the Japanese Ambassador, the negotiations of Ambassador Morris under instructions from the Department and the economic pressure applied by the War Trade Board may be referred to. You should then describe the successful conclusion of these efforts of the United States as evidenced by the arrangements for administration of the railway by Stevens as a Russian employee and the withdrawal of substantial numbers of Japanese troops. We feel that these proceedings and their conclusion can properly be described as a very important and constructive achievement which may be of inestimable value to the people of Russia and to the United States as well as the world in general, provided they are followed through, thereby giving practical effect to the principle of the open door. . . .

. . . The foregoing is designed to indicate the spirit in which the President wishes the Siberian situation to be handled and you should not consider yourself bound to follow literally the suggestions made. It is desired that you treat the matter with the utmost frankness, giving all information at your disposal under, of course, a pledge of confidence. . . .

. . . We feel that it may be a wise practice to take Congress more into confidence on such matters and we at least desire to make the experiment in this case.

Lansing Am[erican] Mission

PRESIDENT WILSON PRESENTS SIBERIAN MILITARY PROBLEMS TO THE COUNCIL OF FOUR

On May 9, 1919, President Wilson, Lloyd George and Clemenceau met at the President's house in Paris to discuss Allied policy in Russia. Wilson presented his dilemma to his colleagues, as summarized below in the notes of the meeting.

POLICY IN RUSSIA

3. PRESIDENT WILSON presented a military problem to his colleagues. The United States, he said, as agreed between the Allied and Associated Powers some time back, had been trying to send supplies to the Civilian population of Siberia from Vladivostok. By agreement between the Allies and a Mr. Stevens, who, long ago in the days of the old regime had been in Siberia, had become the head of a somewhat inconvenient Commission to run the railroads of Siberia. The United States had agreed to police the railroads as far west as Irkutsk. The position was that the United States Government did not believe in Koltchak. The British and French military representatives in Siberia, however, were supporting him. Koltchak had become irritated by the presence on the railway of United States soldiers, whom he regarded as neutrals. Moreover, the impression had got abroad among the peasants of Siberia that the United States was the standard of a free Government which they ought to imitate. When they saw the attitude of neutrality taken up by the United States soldiers, they thought there must be something wrong with the Government of Koltchak. Further, the Cossacks were out of sympathy with the United States soldiers and he suspected that the Japanese would be glad to have a collision between the Cossacks and American soldiers. As a consequence of this state of affairs the United States Government found itself faced with the two following alternatives:

1. To take sides with Koltchak and send much stronger forces to Siberia.
2. To withdraw.

If the former alternative were adopted and the United States increased their forces it was certain that the Japanese would increase theirs still more. The original agreement had been that the Japanese and the United States should send roughly equivalent forces. When the United States sent 9,000 men the Japanese sent 12,000 men. He had not objected to this slight discrepancy, but the numbers of Japanese had subsequently gone up to 70,000, which had afterwards been reduced to a nominal 30,000. This, however, left a great disproportion. If the United States troops continued merely to guard the railway and to maintain, as it were, a neutral position, he was advised that collisions were bound to occur. If United States soldiers were attacked, it could not be expected that they would do nothing. If they were withdrawn, the field would be left to the Japanese and Koltchak, who was supported by the Allies.

He then read a series of telegrams from General Graves commanding the United

U.S., *Foreign Relations, 1919, Russia*, pp. 345–347.

States forces in Siberia, bearing out the above summary of the position, and pointing out that if the present policy were continued, there would almost certainly be a collision between the United States troops and Russian troops.

Mr. LLOYD GEORGE said that this strengthened his view as to the need of arriving at a policy in regard to Russia. Koltchak was advancing Eastward [*Westward*] at a very remarkable rate. He was in a position either to move Northwards and join hands with the forces based on Archangel, or to march on Moscow.

PRESIDENT WILSON said he had always been of opinion that the proper policy of the Allied and Associated Powers was to clear out of Russia and leave it to the Russians to fight it out among themselves.

Mr. LLOYD GEORGE asked that before a decision should be taken, the Council should hear M. Tchaikowsky.

PRESIDENT WILSON agreed.

Mr. LLOYD GEORGE suggested that President Wilson should send a reply to General Graves asking him to take no action for the moment, as the whole problem was being considered by the Allied and Associated Powers.

PRESIDENT WILSON said the risk of this was that there might be a collision between the United States and Russian troops. He suggested that the Allied and Associated Powers should simultaneously ask Koltchak what his programme was. . . .

PRESIDENT WILSON ON POLITICAL RECOGNITION OF KOLCHAK

On May 26 the Council of Four addressed a formal note to Admiral Kolchak explaining Allied policy toward Russia and making a conditional offer of further assistance if Kolchak would agree to certain Allied conditions. Among the assurances requested were pledges that a freely-elected constituent assembly would be convoked as soon as Kolchak reached Moscow, that no attempt would be made to restore the special class privileges of the Czarist regime, that Russia's debts would be recognized and that the new democratic government of Russia would join the League of Nations. On June 4 Kolchak sent a carefully worded affirmative reply which generally complied with the Allied conditions. His reply was accepted by Wilson, Clemenceau, Lloyd George and Baron Makino. The following message from the American Mission to the Acting Secretary of State explains the American government's policy toward Kolchak.

PARIS, *June 25, 1919, 12 p.m.*

For Polk from Lansing and McCormick.

McCormick has spoken to the President regarding Russian situation. He stated that the telegram to Kolchak does not imply political recognition at the present time by any of the Associated Governments but merely offers of assistance in so far as each government's policy and legislation may permit. The absence of formal recognition will in our

U.S., *Foreign Relations, 1919, Russia*, p. 386.

case prevent [us from] extending credit as suggested in your 2363, June 20, 8 p.m. but anything for which they can devise means of payment may now be furnished the Kolchak forces. On his return the President intends to take up with Congress the entire question of economic support for Russia and particularly that pertaining to the Siberian railroad. He expects to send further military instructions to General Graves.

The President expressed his regret at the interpretation given by the press to the telegram sent by the Associated Governments to Admiral Kolchak as he feared that such interpretation might give rise to false hopes.

AMERICAN MISSION

SECRETARY LANSING SEEKS WITHDRAWAL OF AMERICAN TROOPS FROM RUSSIA

Toward the close of 1919, Secretary Lansing outlined in a letter to President Wilson the reasons for the withdrawal of American forces from Siberia.

WASHINGTON, *December 23, 1919.*

MY DEAR MR. PRESIDENT: I enclose a memorandum which I ask your authority to read to the Japanese Ambassador. It means the withdrawal of all our forces from Siberia. I heartily recommend it for your approval. The Secretary of War has read it and is in thorough accord. He informs me the *Mount Vernon* is now approaching Vladivostok and is large enough to carry all our troops.

The truth of the matter is the simple fact that the Kolchak Government has utterly collapsed; the armies of the Bolsheviki have advanced into Eastern Siberia, where they are reported to be acting with moderation. The people seem to prefer them to the officers of the Kolchak régime. Further, the Bolshevik army is approaching the region where our soldiers are, and contact with them will lead to open hostilities and to many complications. In other words, if we do not withdraw we shall have to wage war against the Bolsheviki.

I ask your early and earnest consideration and your authority to proceed.

Faithfully yours,

ROBERT LANSING

Lansing Papers, II, pp. 392–393.

III. CONFLICTING INTERPRETATIONS

George F. Kennan: AMERICAN TROOPS IN RUSSIA: AID FOR THE CZECHO-SLOVAKS?

George Frost Kennan is a diplomat turned historian. Appointed Ambassador to the U.S.S.R. in 1952, he had previously served as the director of the State Department Policy Planning Staff and as counselor of the Department from 1947 to 1950. Retiring in 1953 from his 27 years in the foreign service as a specialist within the framework of Russian affairs, he became a member, and more recently professor, of the Institute for Advanced Study in Princeton, New Jersey. Kennan has authored several major works including a multi-volume study of Soviet-American relations, 1917–1920. The article selected below represents in somewhat abbreviated form the results of Mr. Kennan's research on American intervention in Russia as presented in several of his other volumes.

IF WE REFLECT today on the psychological background of the great conflict of outlook and aspiration between the United States and the ruling party of the Soviet Union, we see that whereas the bitterness of feeling among Americans relates mainly to things the Soviet government has done since the final phases of World War II, Soviet grievances against the United States have a longer historical background and include the behavior of the United States government around the time of the Russian Revolutions of 1917 and in the years immediately following those events. The Allied military intervention of the years 1918 to 1920, in particular, continues to occupy a prominent position in Soviet memory. It has recently been the subject of a number of works by Soviet historians. It has been repeatedly mentioned, just within the past year, in the statements of leading Soviet personalities. And the dominant theme of all this material has been one of bitter reproach to the United States, as having been a leading instigator and participant in the intervention and as having acted, throughout this episode, from motives which were unworthy in themselves and hostile to the interests of the Russian people.

A clear and authoritative view of the Soviet attitude toward the Allied intervention was presented in the autumn of 1957 in the Theses published by the Central Committee of the Communist Party of the Soviet Union in connection with the forty-year anniversary of the Bolshevik Revolution. These Theses dwelt at length on the intervention and described it as consisting of "military campaigns against our country." Nothing was said to suggest that these expeditions might have been directed to any other purpose. The world war was not mentioned.

When the Bolsheviki assumed power in Petrograd in November, 1917, this event caused great concern in the Allied

From George F. Kennan, "American Troops in Russia," *Atlantic Monthly*, CCIII (January, 1959), pp. 36–42. Copyright © 1958, by The Atlantic Monthly Company, Boston, Mass. Reprinted by permission of the author and The Atlantic Monthly Company.

capitals. The leadership of the Bolshevik Party was known to consist of men who not only professed deepest disapproval and contempt for the ideals of the Western governments and peoples but who also publicly denounced the Allied cause in the war as an unworthy and imperialistic one, called for an immediate cessation of hostilities on terms that meant the abandonment of the stated Western war aims, and made it clear that they were resolved to make peace with the Germans. Within a month of their advent to power they moved to put this resolution into effect by entering into negotiations with the Germans. Coming as it did shortly after the military collapse on the Italian front, and with the German offensive of the following spring already looming ahead, the defection of Russia was a grievous and even heart-rending blow to the Allied cause.

One can have one's own view, in the light of history, as to the soundness of Allied war aims, and hence of Allied reasons for wishing to continue the war, in late 1917. But one cannot judge the people of the past by contemporary insights. It was idle to expect the Western governments and peoples to be anything other than deeply worried by the impending departure of Russia from the ranks of the Allied powers, with the prospects that some two million German soldiers might be transferred from the eastern to the western front and that the great physical resources of Russia might then become available to the German war machine.

In these circumstances, it was natural that Allied statesmen and military leaders should have thought of a possible Allied military action in Russia for the purpose of restoring an eastern front against Germany.

We must remember that the Allies did not regard themselves, in the winter of 1917–1918, as being under any obligation to respect the decision of the Soviet government to take Russia out of the war. They did not regard that government as representative of Russian public opinion. They were aware that it had not been elected to office. The Soviet authorities, furthermore, did not at that time control all the territory of the former Russian Empire; there were regions controlled by elements which still professed loyalty to the Allied cause.

In the winter of 1917–1918, the United States was not yet taking a prominent part in the war and was not participating in the military decisions that governed the Allied war effort. It was primarily the French and British military planners who were interested in the possibility of restoring an eastern front. But France and Britain could spare no troops for this purpose. Therefore they turned to America and to Japan for possible sources of manpower and supply for such a military effort.

In the case of Japan, this suggestion raised very delicate problems. Japan was formally a member of the Allied coalition, though it had taken little active part in the war. The political turmoil in European Russia had now thrown Siberia into a state of chaos and weakness. Japan could scarcely be expected to pass up so favorable an opportunity to improve its situation in Manchuria and Eastern Siberia at Russia's expense and thus to rectify the injustice it considered itself to have suffered in the outcome of the Russian-Japanese War.

So long as Russia had been an ally of the Western Powers, the Western governments could not have encouraged any attempt by Japan to profit from Russia's weakness. But now that Russia was out of the war, now that the seats of power in Petrograd and Moscow had been seized by a political faction hostile to the Allied cause, now that the alternative to Japanese penetration of Russia seemed to many people to be German penetration, the question arose as to whether Japan should not be encouraged to enter Siberia, either in conjunction with other Allied forces or as a mandatory agent for the Allies as a whole. Perhaps — or so it seemed to the French and British military planners — perhaps Japanese forces might even be able to penetrate as far as European Russia and to make enough trouble for the Germans there to cause them to retain at least a substantial portion of their troops on the eastern front.

Throughout the winter of 1917–1918, while the Soviet and German negotiators haggled at Brest-Litovsk over the terms of the separate peace between Germany and Russia, the French and British repeatedly approached the United States government with suggestions along these lines. The American response was consistently negative. Neither President Wilson nor his Secretary of State, Robert Lansing, nor his intimate unofficial adviser, Colonel House, could see any merit in these proposals.

Secretary of State Lansing favored a policy of complete abstention from any interference in Russia. " 'Do nothing' should be our policy," he said to the President in December, 1917, "until the black period of terrorism comes to an end." "This government," he said in January, 1918, "must continue for the present a silent witness of the internal confusion which prevails in Russia."

Colonel House similarly warned the President against any action in Russia. To treat Russia as an enemy would, he said, be sure to throw it into the lap of Germany.

That Wilson shared these views of his advisers is clear beyond question. His position was reflected in a number of official statements of the United States government in the winter and spring of 1918, all of which had his official approval and some of which he drafted personally.

A fair example of these was a communication to the Japanese government, of January 20, 1918, which stated:

the common interests of all the powers at war with Germany demand from them an attitude of sympathy with the Russian people . . . any movement looking towards the occupation of Russian territory would at once be construed as one hostile to Russia and would be likely to unite all factions in Russia against us.

The events of February and March, 1918—the reopening in February of hostilities against Russia by the Germans as a means of bringing pressure in the negotiations, the final signature of the Russian-German peace treaty on March 3, its ratification on March 16, and the opening of the great German offensive on the western front five days later—these events caused the heaviest sort of pressure to be brought on Wilson to change his stand and to sanction an intervention in Siberia by the Japanese. Since the Japanese themselves were not yet ready to take any action independently, and refused to act as mandatory for the Allies generally unless the United States joined in making the request, everything appeared to hang on Wilson's decision.

Despite these pressures, the President remained adamant throughout the winter and spring of the year. The wisdom of intervention, he said in a communication to the Allied governments on March 5, seemed to the United States government to be most questionable. If any action were to be taken by the Japanese, he assumed it would be accompanied by a declaration to the effect that they were acting "as an ally of Russia, in Russia's interest, and with the sole view of holding it safe against Germany." But even with such a declaration, he thought the action would be misinterpreted, that

a hot resentment would be generated in Russia itself, and that the whole action might play into the hands of the enemies of Russia, and particularly of the enemies of the Russian Revolution, for which the Government of the United States entertains the greatest sympathy, in spite of all the unhappiness and misfortune which has for the time being sprung out of it.

In the absence of Wilson's approval the Japanese continued, for the moment, to abstain from action. In April, 1918, in the face of the new German offensive in the west, the French and British military planners conceived a somewhat more elaborate scheme for intervention in Russia. This scheme envisaged Allied landings both at Vladivostok and at the northern ports of European Russia. At Vladivostok it would be the Japanese who would bear the main burden; at Murmansk and Archangel a mixed Allied force, in which the Americans would play a prominent part. The expeditions at these widely separated points would combine with local anti-Bolshevik forces loyal to the Allied cause, would advance toward each other, and would eventually link up, thus creating a solid Allied front from Siberia to the Upper Volga region and forcing the Germans to reconstitute their military position in the east.

This was a wholly impractical plan. There was, as American statesmen repeatedly pointed out, no reason at any time to believe that the Japanese were interested in any objectives further west than Irkutsk or that they could be prevailed upon to send their troops beyond the Trans-Baikal area. The anti-Bolshevik Russians with whom it was proposed to collaborate were far too weak to play anything resembling the role assigned to them in this scheme.

It was obvious at the time that Wilson would never have given his approval to such a plan, and the idea was apparently never made known to him in its entirety. Nevertheless, the French and British military planners did not wait for American approval before going ahead to implement the project to the extent they were able.

Insofar as Siberia was concerned, they could, for the moment, do no more than continue and intensify the pressure on Wilson to agree to a Japanese intervention, and this they did to the best of their ability throughout May and June. But with respect to the northern ports, they proceeded to take action at once. Allied warships had already been stationed at Murmansk for many months; the local Soviet there had adopted an attitude friendly to the Allies; and a few British marines had been landed in March with the full consent of the local authorities. Now, in May, the British sent to Murmansk such few soldiers as they were able to spare, under the command of a general who was supposed eventually to command the entire northern expedition. Since this force was wholly inadequate to the purpose in question, the British approached the United States government with the request that an American contingent also be made available for service at the North Russian ports.

Nothing was said to Wilson, on this occasion, about the plan for penetrating into the interior and linking up with the Siberian intervention. The plan was put to him as merely an arrangement for the defense of the northern ports, particularly Murmansk, against the Germans. He was told that there was danger of the Murmansk Railways being attacked by anti-Communist Finns who were supposed to be under German influence and that the Germans might seize Murmansk and develop the port as a submarine base if the Allies did not take preventative action.

We can see today that these fears were greatly exaggerated. But they were sincerely entertained, at the time, by both British and American representatives in Russia.

In addition, Wilson was given to understand that American troops were needed in the Russian North to protect great quantities of Allied war supplies, said to have accumulated in the ports of that region before the October Revolution. Actually, the overwhelming portion of the stores had already been seized and hauled off to the interior by the Bolsheviki, but neither the British government nor Wilson appears to have been aware of these facts.

Despite all the arguments in favor of intervention, Wilson remained at all times skeptical of the merits of this proposed expedition. But he observed, finally, to his Secretary of War that he felt obliged to do it anyhow because the British and French were pressing it on his attention so hard and he had refused so many of their requests that they were beginning to feel that he was not a good associate, much less a good ally. Opposition was made harder for him by the pro-Allied attitude of the local Soviet at Murmansk and by reports from Allied representatives in Russia that the Soviet government was not really so averse as it pretended to be to the idea of an Allied landing in the North.

Wilson therefore finally replied to the British government, in June, 1918, that while he had no enthusiasm for the scheme, he would abide in this instance by the opinion of Marshal Foch, the Allied commander in chief on the western front. If Foch really thought the requested American battalions would be of more use in Murmansk than in France, they would be sent. Foch, at British urging, confirmed to the President in writing that he approved the diversion of this force. The American units were therefore turned over to the British in England in July and placed under British command, to be used in the Russian North as the British might see fit. This was the origin of America's participation in the northern intervention.

Meanwhile, the situation in Siberia had been drastically altered by the outbreak at the end of May of the conflict between the Czechoslovak Corps and the Bolsheviki. This Czech force was made up largely of men who had been taken prisoner or had deserted from the Austro-Hungarian Army and who were desirous of fighting on the Allied side. In the spring of 1918, the Czech Corps was attempting to make its way from European Russia to the western front via Vladivostok. In April and May, it was strung out in trainloads along the Trans-Siberian Railway all the way from the Ukraine to Vladivostok. As a result of the breakdown of the old Russian Army, the Czech Corps was now probably the strongest single armed force in Russia.

On May 26, hostilities broke out between the Czechs and the Soviet authorities along the route. This uprising of the Czechs was not, as has been frequently alleged, the result of Allied instigation. It was a product of the frictions and misunderstandings occasioned by the effort of the Czechs to move across Siberia in the chaotic conditions then existing, and especially of the incidents which occurred when the Czechs encountered parties of Austrian or Hungarian war prisoners who were, after the conclusion of the Brest-Litovsk peace, due for repatriation and were trying to make their way along the railway in the opposite direction.

Not only were the French and British not responsible for the Czech uprising, but the uprising actually came as a set-back to the Allied military planners, who had hoped to use a portion of the Czech Corps in the northern ports and had just made arrangements with the Soviet authorities to have this portion of the corps routed to the Russian North. The outbreak of the conflict between the Czechs and the Bolsheviki made this impossible, and the failure of the Czechs ever to arrive at Archangel had a good deal to do with the eventual failure of the northern expedition.

As a result of their uprising, the Czechs were successful in seizing, within a few days, most of the Trans-Siberian Railway from the Volga to Irkutsk. Another body of some eighteen thousand Czechs had by this time arrived at Vladivostok, but there were, at the time of the uprising, no Czech trains in the area between Vladivostok and Irkutsk. This territory thus remained initially in Soviet hands.

The Czechs in Vladivostok were now concerned to re-establish contact with their compatriots in Central and Western Siberia and to ensure the security of the passage of the main body of the corps to the Pacific. To this end, they seized Vladivostok at the end of June and mounted an operation westward to clear the railway toward Irkutsk. Finding themselves opposed by Communist forces in the neighborhood of Vladivostok, they appealed to the Allied governments and particularly to the Japanese and United States governments for military support. In doing so, they contrived to convey to official Washington the impression that the opposition with which they found themselves faced was provided not by Russian Communists but by German and Austrian prisoners of war who had been rearmed by the Bolsheviki and who now threatened to seize Siberia on behalf of the Central Powers.

Again, this was a very distorted impression. We know today that very few of the war prisoners in Siberia—two or three thousand at the most out of some eight hundred thousand—were armed by the Bolsheviki. These were all prisoners who had accepted the Communist orientation. They were mostly Hungarians. There were scarcely any Germans among them. Neither the German nor the Austrian government had had anything to do with the rearming of these men; both governments had in fact opposed it vigorously. But the myth of Siberia's being about to be seized by Germany through the agency of the war prisoners was diligently propagated by all those Allied officials, particularly the French, who wanted intervention; and the Czechs, who were now very anxious for American support, did not hesitate to avail themselves, sincerely or otherwise, of the same suggestion.

To Wilson, this apparent plight of the Czechs presented a wholly new situation. Here was an Allied force, apparently fighting to keep Siberia out of German hands, and it needed American support. Wilson had extremely friendly feelings for the Czechs, as he did for the other Slavic peoples of Eastern Europe. And he had, like many other Americans, a sentimental prejudice in favor of little countries. Little countries, he thought, were good; big countries (aside from his own) were bad. Thus the plight of the Czechs as he understood it appealed to him, and he thought he saw in it at long last a possibility for putting an end to the pressures of the British and French for action in Siberia without associating himself with their political schemes, of which he was deeply suspicious. He therefore arrived, on July 6, 1918, at his final decision. The text of it, as recorded in a confidential cabinet document, is now available. Wilson wrote every word of it himself.

In this memorandum, the President once again dismissed emphatically the whole idea of attempting to restore an eastern front against Germany by an action through Siberia. With this he would have nothing to do. But he did see justification for helping the Czechoslovaks at Vladivostok to establish contact with their compatriots further west. He was prepared, he said, to send seven thousand American soldiers, provided that the Japanese would put up a similar force, to guard the line of communication of the Vladivostok Czechs as they advanced westward along the Trans-Siberian Railway to make contact with their comrades at Irkutsk.

Wilson's decision has often been portrayed as part of a general Allied decision for intervention in Siberia. Actually, it was not this at all. It was in no way responsive to what the British and French had been urging on him, and he did not regard it as being so. He did not consider the action he was authorizing to be intervention against the Bolsheviki, and in communicating his decision to the other Allied governments he condemned the very idea of intervention in the roundest of terms. The British were furious with him over the whole affair; they regarded his decision as a unilateral one, not in any way responsive to their request, and in answer to it they proceeded to act on their own, with a view to realizing the plans they had conceived.

The Japanese, who were thrown into a great crisis of decision by Wilson's proposal, also proceeded after some hesitation to take what was virtually unilateral action, although they tried to present it as a response to Wilson's initiative. They sent to Siberia an expedition far greater than anything Wilson had proposed, and in conjunction with this they seized Northern Manchuria, an act which the United States government greatly deplored. At one moment, Wilson was inclined to withdraw from the entire undertaking, but it was too late. He realized that to withdraw would be to give the Japanese a free hand in Siberia and to forfeit all possibility of exercising any restraining influence on them by maintaining the semblance of Allied collaboration. The American force was therefore sent, as proposed.

So much for the origins of the American action in Russia. Now a word about the course it took. It is necessary to distinguish these two things quite sharply, for in both instances—North Russia and Siberia—the President's decision was taken against an inaccurate pattern of information, partly out of date, partly erroneous; and in neither case did the actual course of events resemble in any way what he had hoped would be the result of his decision.

The three battalions destined for service in the Russian North were turned over to the British in England in midsummer of 1918. Their fate was now in British hands. They were young recruits, mostly of Polish-American origin, from Michigan and Wisconsin. They had had very little training, no combat experience, and no political indoctrination whatsoever. I do not believe that one out of a hundred of them had the faintest idea why they were being sent to North Russia or against whom they were supposed to be acting. Equipped with British uniforms and Russian rifles, they were loaded onto troopships and dispatched northward at the end of August. The Spanish influenza broke out on board all three vessels. Medical supplies were not available. Both men and crews were decimated.

The British, meanwhile, without awaiting the arrival of the Americans, had landed at Archangel with a small, inadequate force, consisting mainly of some six hundred British and one French colonial battalion. The Archangel Soviet, in contrast to that of Murmansk, was not friendly to the Allies, and the bloodless entry of the Allied force was made possible only by a *putsch* carried out in the city by anti-Communist elements on the eve of the arrival of the Allied expedition. But the Bolsheviki mounted resistance on the outskirts of the city, and the British soon found themselves hard pressed even to maintain a perimeter some hundred kilometers from the center of the place. The American units, which were originally assigned to Murmansk, were therefore hastily rerouted to Archangel, where they arrived on September 4. Of those who were healthy, the majority were packed off the same evening for the front. By the next day, they found themselves deep in the swamps and forests of Northern Russia, under fire for the first time in their lives, and facing an adversary of whose identity they had no clear idea.

In the ensuing weeks and months, things developed in a highly unfavorable and unexpected way in the area held by the Allies around Archangel. The anti-Communist Russians within the Allied perimeter fell into two main categories: the Social Revolutionaries and the conservative former officers. These two factions loathed each other as violently as they did the Bolsheviki, and agreed on

nothing. Their squabbles, superimposed on a complete lack of unity and of political understanding among the Allied representatives themselves, disgusted and antagonized the local population. It proved impossible to recruit any sizable and reliable Russian armed force. With the few foreign troops he had at his disposal, the British commander was able to do no more than to hold on to his perimeter around the city. The early descent of the arctic winter pinned the troops to their defensive positions, and any deep advance into the interior became out of the question.

In Siberia, things were no better. There, too, the Americans arrived in September. The junction of the Vladivostok Czechs with those on the western reaches of the Trans-Siberian Railway had, ironically enough, been effected on the day prior to the arrival of the main body of the Americans. The Czechs, furthermore, had decided, under Allied encouragement, not to try to make their way out of Russia through Vladivostok but rather to remain in Siberia and to fight the Bolsheviki in the area of the Urals. But the Japanese were now in Siberia, with ten times the number of troops Wilson had envisaged. No one wanted to leave the field entirely to them.

The Americans therefore settled down to guarding sections of the Amur Railway thousands of miles from any place where fighting was going on in the Russian civil war. It does not appear that any of these American forces ever fired a shot in regular combat against any unit of the Red Army during the year and a half of their stay in Siberia. There was one advance contingent of the Americans who, before the arrival of the American general, allowed themselves to be taken under Japanese command and were thus included, though not on the firing line, among the forces used in one small battle between the Japanese and the Czechs on the one hand and the Communists on the other. The American commander, General Graves, who arrived a few days later, put a stop to this use of his men. Graves was a fine soldier with an iron-clad sense of duty. He took very seriously the President's injunction that he was not to get mixed up in Russian politics. He was extremely unpopular with the Allied representatives in Siberia, precisely for his firm refusal to participate in any action against the Bolsheviki or against any other Russian faction as such, and there were even charges from the British and French side that he was pro-Bolshevik.

Only a few weeks after the arrival of these American units in North Russia and Siberia World War I came to an end. This rendered unsubstantial the main military objectives for which the expeditions had been dispatched and raised the question of what should be done with them. In view of the fact that the situation in Russia was certain to be one of the first subjects for discussion among the senior Allied statesmen at the forthcoming Paris Peace Conference, no action was taken regarding the Allied forces in Russia in the initial weeks following the armistice.

At Paris, the whole question of Russia and the intervention was repeatedly discussed by the senior Allied figures. Wilson came to the conference convinced that the Allied intervention in Russia was a mistake and a failure. The Allied forces there, he said at one of the sessions of the Council of Ten in February, 1919, were doing no good. They did not know for whom or for what they were fighting. They were not assisting any promising common effort to establish order. They ought to be removed at once.

This remained his opinion throughout,

and as soon as it became clear that the Peace Conference could find no useful action to take in the Russian problem as a whole, the British government was advised that the United States government desired that the American forces in North Russia should leave at the earliest opportunity. This could not be before late spring or early summer, owing to the ice conditions in the approaches to Archangel. Also, the United States government had no inclination to pull the troops out so abruptly as to cause military embarrassment to those Allied forces with whom they had been associated. They actually left Northern Russia in June and July, 1919, which was just about as soon as their departure could be decently arranged.

In the nine or ten months of their service on Russian soil, these Americans had taken no part in any actions other than ones of a defensive nature. Even this they had done under British command, and in the execution of a scheme which their President had never understood or sanctioned. They were a small force, three or four thousand men in all. Their withdrawal had nothing to do with any defeat in battle.

In Siberia, the situation of the American force was complicated by the fact that during the winter of 1919, before and during the Paris Peace Conference, the French and British succeeded in bringing about the establishment in Central and Western Siberia of an anti-Bolshevik authority under Admiral Kolchak. The Americans, who had nothing to do with this development, found themselves in effect guarding Kolchak's line of communication, or at least a small portion of it, far from the front. As the Peace Conference neared its end, reports were received in Paris that the Kolchak forces were doing well in their struggle against the Bolsheviki, and heavy pressure was brought to bear on Wilson, both by the British and by subordinates in his own American establishment, to give recognition and support to the Kolchak cause. Wilson authorized an investigation of Kolchak's situation, and pending the outcome of this investigation, he delayed the removal of the American force in Eastern Siberia. The investigation was not completed until late summer. It revealed that Kolchak was not doing well at all; he was doing so badly, in fact, that nothing short of a rescue expedition in the number of fifty thousand Allied troops could save him. Anything of this sort was out of the question.

By the time this report was received in Washington, Wilson was already embarked on his tragic speaking tour, trying to assure American ratification of the peace treaty and membership in the League of Nations. In the course of this tour he suffered a stroke, and he was never able fully to resume his control of American policy.

With Kolchak's defeat in the late autumn of 1919, it became clear that the American force could no longer be left in Siberia without danger of its becoming seriously embroiled in the Russian civil war. The decision to withdraw it was therefore taken, in the early winter of 1920, and the troops were removed as soon as this could be physically arranged, which was in April.

In 1933, when negotiations were undertaken between the United States and the Soviet Union looking toward a resumption of diplomatic relations, the Soviet negotiator, Litvinov, arrived in Washington prepared to advance a major claim against the United States government for damages allegedly done by the Americans in the course of the Siberian intervention. He was then permitted by the United States government to see certain of the materials in the American archives dealing with this subject. After examining these materials and communicating with his government, Litvinov addressed a letter to President Roosevelt formally renouncing, on behalf of the Soviet government, any claim for damages arising out of the American expedition in Siberia. The matter has never, to my knowledge, been officially raised since that time, though the Communist propaganda machine has worked the issue for all it was worth.

Viewed in their entirety, the American expeditions to North Russia and Siberia appear today as pathetic and ill-conconceived ventures, to which Woodrow Wilson, poorly informed, harried with wartime burdens, and torn between his own instincts and his feeling of obligation to his Allies—was brought against his own better judgment. He did his best at all times to keep the American action from assuming the form of an interference in Russian internal affairs, and there is no suggestion more preposterous than that he was animated in these decisions by hostility toward the Russian people or by a desire to overthrow the Soviet regime with American forces. In both cases, his original decision was closely linked with America's wartime concerns. Had there been no great European war in progress, neither expedition would ever have been dispatched.

That the expeditions were regrettable —that it would have been better, from the standpoint of American interests, had they never been sent—seems hardly open to doubt. That they reflected imperialistic motives and constituted a serious injury to the Russian people is a figment of the imagination of Soviet propagandists, useful to their political purpose but not to the development of historical truth.

Betty Miller Unterberger: AMERICAN INTERVENTION: A BRAKE ON THE ALLIES?

Betty Miller Unterberger, professor of history at Texas A. & M. University, authored the first full-length study of America's Siberian expedition as an exploration in national policy. The piece selected below, drawn from two articles, explores the origin of President Wilson's decision to send troops to Siberia and examines the actual operation of the policy in Siberia.

DURING THE FIRST six months of 1918 President Wilson was besieged with appeals for military intervention in Siberia. They came from his Allies and the Supreme War Council, and also from his own diplomatic staff abroad. Although the cry for intervention was practically unanimous among American foreign representatives in Russia and the Far East, Wilson found a strong resistance among his military advisers. Wilson, indeed, faced one of the most difficult problems of his career; he informed Colonel Edward M. House that he was "sweating blood" over it. As the Russo-German peace negotiations at Brest-Litovsk neared their conclusion in March, 1918, and the Germans withdrew an increasing number of divisions from their Russian front, Britain and France increased their pressure for intervention. The Allies faced what appeared to be a desperate military situation. In the early part of the year they were ready to clutch at every straw. General Tasker H. Bliss, American military representative on the Supreme War Council, later pointed out that the Siberian expedition was a "side-show born of desperation." Thus the original idea of intervention was not primarily to initiate a war against Bolshevism, but to bring about a renewal of the Russian thrust against eastern Germany.

As early as December 14, 1917, the British ambassador in Japan had discussed informally with the Japanese government the problem of protecting the Amur and Trans-Siberian railways and the stores and munitions at Vladivostok. The American government was not informed of these discussions, which resulted in the sending of warships to Vladivostok. By January 17, 1918, the Japanese had sent four ships, and the British, one. Josephus Daniels, the American Secretary of the Navy, felt this was cause for concern. He suggested that Japan be informed that the United States thought "it a mistake to create the impression they intended to land." He also advised the dispatch of the cruiser *Brooklyn* to Vladivostok.

The Japanese government raised no objection to the sending of the *Brooklyn*, but it requested that "if conditions should hereafter require the occupation of Vladivostok and the lines of the Chinese Eastern and Amur Railways . . . that this task be left to her alone." Japan had asked the British government to agree to this as evidence of confidence in her good faith. This request, in conjunction with the large naval force at Vladivostok, gave Wilson an "uncomfortable feeling." Since the suggestion seemed to him to be "very significant of possible coming events," he

From Betty Miller Unterberger, "President Wilson and the Decision to Send American Troops to Siberia," *Pacific Historical Review*, XXIV (February, 1955), pp. 63–74. Reprinted by permission of *Pacific Historical Review*.

insisted that Japan be told very clearly that the United States would strongly disapprove of military action in that area.

In January, 1918, the British government suggested that Japan be invited to occupy the Trans-Siberian Railway as the mandatory of the Allies, in order to keep open a line of communication with the Russian forces in the south and southeast who wanted to continue the war against Germany. The President was strongly opposed to the suggested expedition. He had reason to believe that it was the Japanese who had originated the plan for invading Siberia, and that they wished the expedition to be exclusively Japanese in order to secure control of the maritime provinces. Wilson intended to prevent such a development.

Arthur Balfour, the British Foreign Minister, admitted that it might be impossible to get Japan out of the maritime provinces if she once got established there, but he added "the Japanese occupation of the Maritime Provinces is a question which must probably be faced in any case as the state of Russia will probably soon render occupation inevitable. Japan in such circumstances will doubtless take action on her own initiative, whatever the wishes of the Allies will be."

Wilson could see nothing "wise or practicable" in the scheme. It seemed to him "unwise to make a request which would in itself give the Japanese a certain moral advantage with respect to any ultimate desires or purposes she may have with regard to the eastern province of Siberia." On February 8, the State Department formally and pointedly rejected the British proposals. Furthermore, it indicated that if future conditions should warrant the occupation of the whole or part of the Trans-Siberian Railway, it should be done through international cooperation

and not by any one power acting as the mandatory of the others. Two further appeals, one from the British Foreign Office and one from Balfour, evoked no change in this attitude. Shortly thereafter, arrangements were made with Boris Bakhmetev, Russian Ambassador to the United States from the defunct provisional government, to continue the original plan for sending the Russian Railway Service Corps into Siberia. This corps of American engineers had been organized at the request of the provisional government in September of 1917 for the purpose of aiding in the rehabilitation of the Trans-Siberian and Chinese Eastern railways. The corps was now authorized to begin work in cooperation with the railway authorities of the Chinese Eastern Railway and operate eastward toward Vladivostok and westward gradually to Irkutsk. It was from this date and throughout 1918 that the Japanese and American governments waged a diplomatic duel over the control of the Chinese Eastern Railway.

During the next few weeks Wilson was overwhelmed with appeals for intervention from his Allies, from the Supreme War Council, and from Ferdinand Foch, Generalissimo of the Allied Armies. From Versailles, Bliss reported a feeling of "desperation" in regard to the war. He urged Washington to bear this in mind as a probable explanation for such proposals as Japanese intervention.

On February 27, 1918, the President received a secret message from Balfour, which urged that Japan be invited to occupy the Siberian railway in order to protect the Allied military stores lying at Vladivostok and to prevent the enemy from gaining access to the vast agricultural resources available to the west of Lake Baikal. Great Britain admitted reluctantly that although Japan desired a mandatory, she would not tolerate co-operation. France was eager for the decision. Italy approved of the project. The final decision rested with the United States.

Wilson found it very difficult to resist these appeals. Too often he had found himself opposing Allied schemes. Now, he found himself again in the position of refusing to agree to a plan which had the support of all the Allies. Reluctantly, he decided to agree to Japanese intervention without American participation. He drafted a new declaration of policy stating that although "the United States has not thought it wise to join the governments of the Entente in asking the Japanese government to act in Siberia," it would not object to such a request being made by the other Allies. On March 1, Wilson sent this statement to the State Department for the information of the Allied ambassadors.

As soon as the Russian ambassador in Washington learned of the proposed note, he informed House that the Russians preferred the Germans to the Japanese, and that a Japanese expeditionary force would throw the Russians into the arms of the Germans. House informed Wilson of the Russian ambassador's views, and wrote in opposition to Japanese action:

We are treading upon exceedingly delicate and dangerous ground, and are likely to lose that fine moral position you have given the Entente cause. . . . I cannot understand the determination of the British and French to urge the Japanese to take such a step. Leaving out the loss of moral advantage, it it doubtful whether there will be any material gain.

House's letter was followed by one from William C. Bullitt, who stressed the point that America's position would be irretrievably compromised unless the United States protested publicly against Japan's invasion of Siberia. He pointed out that Japan wanted to annex eastern Siberia, and that the Allies and the United States realized it. He continued with a moving plea:

The President must oppose invasion of Siberia by Japan in the name of democracy and liberalism. He must act, or his position as moral leader of the liberals of the world will be lost. We cannot wash our hands of this matter. Unless we oppose, we assent.

Influenced by the views of House and Bullitt, Wilson reverted to his earlier stand on intervention. He drafted a new note which clearly revealed his concern over the moral issues involved in intervention. It rested the case against intervention upon two assumptions: first, that such a policy would strengthen the extreme revolutionary elements in Russia and would alienate Russian opinion from faith in the Allies and America; second, that the course proposed was contrary to America's democratic war aims and would fatally compromise the American moral position.

Although rebuffed by Wilson's opposition, the British soon devised a new plan of action. They proposed that an inter-Allied expedition of American, British, and Japanese troops be substituted for lone Japanese intervention. By this scheme, they hoped to overcome not only Bolshevik objections to military action in Siberia, but also Wilson's opposition. House was quite sympathetic to the new proposal, and agreed that many of the disadvantages of intervention would disappear if it could be put upon an inter-Allied basis and that they might all disappear if an invitation could be secured from Trotsky.

One of the main reasons for the American refusal to intervene in Siberia was that no invitation was forthcoming from the Russians. The British, therefore, were attempting to persuade the Soviet authorities to participate in the war against Germany with Allied military assistance. Lord Reading, British ambassador in Washington, admitted the possibility that British negotiations might constitute a recognition of the Soviet regime. However, he believed that such a course was justified if it secured President Wilson's approval of inter-Allied action in Siberia. As the Assistant Secretary of State pointed out, "The British are trying to create a situation in Siberia to suit the President, even though in so doing, they may be obliged to come to some form of agreement with the Soviets."

Although the State Department was opposed to intervention by Japan alone, it had not given up consideration of an Allied intervention. This was indicated by a significant event. The Italian and Belgian governments requested the United States War Department to aid in transporting some of their troops from the Far East to Europe. The State Department advised the withdrawal of these requests. The Department deemed it advisable that "as many as possible of the governments at war with Germany should be temporarily represented by military forces in the Far East." If Allied troops were withdrawn "it might be embarrassing to send back there other such troops."

Throughout 1918 the threatened activities of Austro-German war prisoners were a vital factor in the Allied pleas for intervention. By the end of March the persistent reports of armed and organized prisoners in Siberia caused Lansing considerable worry. He felt that if the Germans became masters of Irkutsk they might invade Manchuria and obtain control of the Trans-Siberian Railway. If these reports were true he did not see how Japan could be expected to refrain from taking action in Siberia in resistance to the German advance. Perhaps in the circumstances, it might even be wise to sanction Japan's entry into Siberia as the mandatory of the Allies. Although the accuracy of these various reports was never fully determined, the general tendency among the Allies was to accept them at face value. Certainly they influenced Wilson's final decision in favor of intervention.

By the end of May, the United States had good reason to suspect that Japan was ready to act independently in the Far East. She had concluded a military agreement with China, and was wholeheartedly supporting Captain Gregorii Semenov, one of the anti-Bolshevik leaders in eastern Siberia. Paul S. Reinsch, the American minister to China, began to demand Allied action, fearing that delay was dangerous.

As early as February 23, the State Department had been aware that negotiations for a military agreement had been in progress. Reinsch had then informed Lansing that Japan had proposed to China that the two nations cooperate "in restoring order in Siberia." China had turned to the United States for advice on the matter. Lansing found it difficult to protest against the measures since they were ostensibly aimed at a common foe. He did, however, advise the Chinese government that if Japan deemed military occupation a necessity, China should guard the Chinese Eastern Railway.

The Military Agreements of May 16 and 19, signed in Peking by the military authorities of Japan and China, provided for Sino-Japanese military and naval cooperation in the event that their territories or "the general peace and tranquility in the extreme Orient should be menaced by the enemy." Admiral Aleksander Kolchak, who had arrived in Siberia for the purpose of setting up an anti-Bolshevik government and was well acquainted with Japanese methods, expressed the belief that Japan had obtained the "approval of China to bring Japanese forces into north Manchuria and ultimately secure complete control" of the region.

This was exactly what Wilson hoped to prevent. He wished to preserve the open door in Siberia and North Manchuria, without interfering in the factional disputes of the Russians. He had ordered the Russian Railway Service Corps to begin work along the line of the Chinese Eastern Railway primarily to prevent the Japanese from assuming control. However, he did inform John F. Stevens, head of the Russian Railway Advisory Mission, that the corps of American engineers should not

be drawn in to take sides in a movement which partakes of civil war, consequently, their work on the Chinese Eastern Railway must not have any semblance of supporting Semenov or contributing to the success of his military operations. If this can only be accomplished by their withdrawal then they should be withdrawn.

While the Sino-Japanese negotiations were in progress, the Supreme War Council was expending much energy trying to launch the Siberian expedition. This time the Allies tried a new approach; they determined to ask Japan for certain guarantees in advance of intervention, in order to remove Wilson's objections to the proposed expedition. Bliss cabled immediately for instructions in regard to these proposals. General Peyton C. March, Chief of Staff, stated the President's views in forceful language:

The President's attitude is that Russia's misfortune imposes upon us at this time the obligation of unswerving fidelity to the principle of Russian territorial integrity and political independence. Intervention via Vladivostok is deemed impracticable because of the vast distance involved, and the size of the force necessary to be effective, and financing such an expedition would mean burdens which the United States at this time ought not to assume. . . . The idea of compensating Japan by territory in Asiatic Russia is inadmissible.

In March, a force of some seventy thousand Czechoslovaks had started across Siberia to Vladivostok with the consent of the Bolshevik government. From Vladivostok, they expected to be transported to France to fight on the Western Front. William Phillips, Assistant Secretary of State, suggested the advisability of retaining the Czechs in Siberia "pending the development of the situation on the eastern front where they may be needed to reinforce possible Russian opposition to further incroachments by Germany." Both Basil Miles, acting chief of the Russian Division, and Joseph C. Grew, acting chief of the Western European Division, agreed that the retention of the Czechs would be highly desirable, but "to go on record as recommending it to the British Government might prove embarrassing in connection with our attitude toward Japanese intervention." These exchanges indicated that the State Department had begun to think in terms of Allied intervention.

While the President struggled to a decision on intervention, relations between the Czechs and Bolsheviks had been strained to the breaking point. By the end of May, fighting broke out between the two groups in central and western Siberia. As a result, the Czechs in Vladivostok feared for the safe exit of their brothers from the interior, and on June 20, they decided to act. They placed guards over the military stores in Vladivostok to prevent their shipment west, and determined to return to rescue the Czechs in central and western Siberia from the armed war prisoners and Bolsheviks. At the same time members of the Czech National Council in Vladivostok appealed to the Allied consuls for a supporting force of "from 50,000 to 100,000 Allied troops to establish a permanent front against Germany."

Lansing believed that the Czech situation had created a new condition which should receive careful consideration. He asked Wilson to consider the possibility of using the Czech troops as a nucleus for the military occupation of the Trans-Siberian Railway. Minister Reinsch was also urging the utilization of the Czechs. He had written:

It is the general opinion of Allied representatives here in which I concur that it would be a serious mistake to remove the Czecho-Slovak troops from Siberia. With only slight countenance and support they could control all of Siberia against the Germans. They are sympathetic to the Russian population, eager to be accessories to the Allied cause, the most serious means [menace] to extension of German influence in Russia. Their removal would greatly benefit Germany and further discourage Russia. If they were not in Siberia it would be worth while to bring them there from a distance.

Wilson was profoundly impressed by the suggestion from Reinsch. He wrote Lansing: "There seems to me to emerge from this suggestion the shadow of a plan that might be worked with Japanese and other assistance. These people [the Czechoslovaks] are the cousins of the Russians."

As the month of June ended, events seemed to be forcing the President's hand. All his Allies as well as the vast majority of his diplomatic advisers at home and abroad were urging action. In addition, the threat of independent action loomed on the horizon. The machinery for such action had already been provided by the Sino-Japanese Military Agreements of May, 1918. The Czechs, who had taken over control of Vladivostok and strategic terminals along the Trans-Siberian Railway, appeared ready and willing to remain in Siberia, if the Allies desired it. The decision apparently rested with the President.

On July 2 the Supreme War Council sent the President an urgent appeal for intervention in Siberia. By July 3 Wilson's mind was "crystallizing" in the direction of an economic commission accompanied by an armed protective force. Lord Reading believed that "the addition of the Czecho-slovak incidents in Vladivostok and elsewhere and the resolution of the Supreme War Council endorsed by General Foch" would "cause him to decide in favor of a military force accompanying the Commission and of a more important character than he had originally intended."

On July 6 the President decided to act. He announced his decision to embark upon an expedition in cooperation with Japan. He agreed with his military advisers that the establishment of an Eastern Front was militarily unfeasible. Therefore, he refused to consider any advance westward beyond Irkutsk. Military action in Russia was admissible only to help the "Czecho-slovaks consolidate their forces and get into successful cooperation with their Slavic kinsmen and to steady any efforts at self-government or self-defense in which the Russians themselves may be willing to accept assistance."

On July 17 Wilson delivered an *aide mémoire* to the Allied ambassadors which defined the objectives of America's proposed expedition to Siberia. He proposed to ask all nations associated in the American program to unite

in assuring the people of Russia in the most public and solemn manner that none of the governments uniting in action either in Siberia or in northern Russia contemplates any interference of any kind with the political sovereignty of Russia, any intervention in her internal affairs, or any impairment of her territorial integrity either now or hereafter, but that each of the associated powers has the single object of affording such aid as shall be acceptable, and only such aid as shall be acceptable, to the Russian people in their endeavor to regain control of their own affairs, their own territory, and their own destiny.

Wilson's decision to intervene in Siberia was based on several reasons. He had placed the winning of the war first. This implied no quarrel with the Allies. When the Allies insisted on going into Siberia, he had finally yielded on the theory that if he participated in the venture, he would later be able to say, "Now let us come out," instead of, "Now you come out." He made his decision after it was clear that intervention would take place despite his opposition and probably with Japan in charge of the expedition. When it became evident that Japan was prepared to embark upon an independent expedition under the auspices of the Sino-Japanese Military Agreements of May, 1918, Wilson invited Japan to participate in a joint expedition to Siberia. He did so, however, not because he believed in the expedition, but because he thought he could

"impose greater restraint on Japan within rather than outside of it." The guiding motive of American policy in Siberia and North Manchuria was the maintenance of the open door free from Japanese imperialistic designs.

* * *

The month following Wilson's decision was spent in a useless endeavor to get Japan to agree to the principle of "joint equal military action." Despite the State Department's agreement to permit the Japanese to have the high command in return for a definite limitation on the numbers of Japanese troops to be sent to Siberia, the final Japanese declaration failed to mention the number of troops participating in the venture. Moreover, the Japanese ambassador made it clear that in the event of an emergency, Japan might be forced to send additional troops "without consultation."

Before the United States had completed its negotiations with Japan, the British, French, Italians and Chinese indicated their intentions to participate in the expedition. Actually, Wilson did not want the participation of Great Britain or France. He had opposed the secret support and encouragement given to factions in various parts of Russia. Lansing expressed the President's views when he pointed out: "The participation of these two Governments will give the enterprise the character of interference with the domestic affairs of Russia and create the impression that the underlying purpose is to set up a new pro-Ally Government in Siberia, if not in Russia."

Immediately upon the arrival of troops in Siberia, the divergence of views concerning the purpose of intervention be-

From Betty Miller Unterberger, "The Russian Revolution and Wilson's Far-Eastern Policy," *The Russian Review*, XVI (April 1957), pp. 37–46. Reprinted by permission of *The Russian Review*.

came clearly apparent. While Great Britain and France attempted to extend the scope of military and political action in Siberia, and Japan proceeded with her plans to occupy Manchuria and the Russian Far East, the United States spent its efforts attempting to limit and restrain the independent operations of its Allies.

No sooner had Wilson announced his decision to send an expedition to Siberia than Britain and France sought his cooperation in the establishment of a unified political control of affairs in Siberia. Wilson agreed with Secretary Lansing that these efforts were "simply another move to impress our action in Siberia with the character of intervention rather than relief of the Czechs." When the French suggested that an American High Commissioner be appointed as head of an inter-Allied civilian board, Lansing dismissed the proposal as "bait to draw us into a policy which has been so insistently urged by Great Britain for the past six months."

Wilson agreed. He revealed his anxiety in a letter to Lansing.

The other governments are going much further than we — and much faster — are, indeed, acting upon a plan which is altogether foreign from ours and inconsistent with it. Please make plain to the French Ambassador that we do not think cooperation in *political* action necessary or desirable in eastern Siberia because we contemplate no political action of any kind there, but only the action of friends who stand at hand and wait to see how they can help. The more plain and emphatic that is made, the less danger will there be of (or?) subsequent misunderstandings and irritations.

American troops had scarcely arrived in Siberia when the British government requested that additional troops be sent. The French made a similar request.

When the State Department made clear its opposition to such a proposal, the British suggested that the State Department formally request the Japanese government to dispatch the necessary military assistance.

The President was clearly disturbed by the efforts of his Allies to enlarge the size of the expedition to Siberia. He was concerned because the Czechs were making no attempt to retire. The British ambassador soon found that the President was

. . . beginning to feel that the Allies are trying to rush, even trick, him into a policy which he had refused to accept. He is well aware that he is committed to the task of rescuing the Czechs, but thinks the Allies are already trying to change the character of the expedition into a full-fledged military intervention with the object of reconstituting the Eastern Front.

Meanwhile, the Czech leaders were pleading for immediate assistance. Without such assistance, they would be forced to retire east of the Ural Mountains. They were opposed to such a retreat because it would leave defenseless those Russians who had supported them against the Bolsheviks.

The President made his position quite clear. If the Czechs desired American cooperation, they must retire to the eastern side of the Urals. The United States would "not be a party to any attempt to form an Eastern front."

All the Allied governments were informed accordingly. Great Britain immediately replied that the decision to hold American troops in Eastern Siberia would not affect her determination to aid the Czechs in holding their position west of the Urals. She felt obligated to assist those Russians who had been loyal allies throughout the war. She intended not only to continue her efforts in their behalf but also to request the French and Japanese governments to follow British policy in standing by the "loyal" Russians against the Bolsheviks.

Actually, Japan had no desire to cooperate in any military activities west of the Ural Mountains. Her designs were concerned primarily with Eastern Siberia and North Manchuria. Thus, she was quite willing to agree with the American position.

While Washington resisted Anglo-French efforts to broaden the scope of the Siberian expedition, Tokyo was proceeding along its own independent course. Expressing its concern over the "invasion of Chinese territory by Bolsheviks and organized German war prisoners," the Japanese government indicated its intention to send an independent Japanese force to protect the Manchurian border, this despite China's repeated and emphatic denials that its borders had been violated by Bolsheviks or German prisoners of war.

By August 21, the Japanese had stationed twelve thousand troops along the line of the Chinese Eastern Railway. A few days later Tokyo announced its intention to send ten thousand additional troops to the Maritime Province. Its justification for such action was the critical situation of the Czechs, the increased activity of armed German war prisoners, and pressure by the European Allies as well as the Czechs.

Japan continued to pour troops into Siberia. By the time the Armistice was signed on November 11, 1918, she had sent three divisions, or some seventy thousand men, all of them under the direct control of the General Staff in Tokyo. The Japanese occupation of Eastern Siberia was quite thorough. The whole operation was aptly described as "a commercial invasion under military convoy."

Once Japanese troops began to pour into Siberia and North Manchuria, the State Department became convinced that Japan would succeed in gaining control of the railways unless the United States took a firm stand. On November 16, 1918, Secretary Lansing made the first of numerous representations to Tokyo concerning Japanese actions. The United States protested against the number of Japanese troops in Eastern Asia and the monopoly of control which they exercised there. The State Department recommended that the railways be placed under military control and operated by the Russian Railway Service Corps, a body of American engineers dispatched at the request of the Provisional Government in September, 1917, to operate the Trans-Siberian Railway.

Japan formally rejected the American railway plan, and Japanese military authorities proceeded with their efforts to take over the management and control of the Chinese Eastern Railway. The United States, however, continued to insist that inter-Allied, not exclusive Japanese control, be maintained on the railways.

After a month of patient negotiation and an internal struggle within the Japanese government, an inter-Allied railway agreement was finally reached. Simultaneously, Japan announced the withdrawal of thirty thousand troops from Manchuria. Premier Takashi Hara, who had assumed office in September, had been trying to free the Japanese government from the domination of the General Staff. It was obvious that he had won an initial victory over the reactionary military forces.

The Inter-Allied Railway Agreement of January 9, 1919, provided that the operation of the railroads under Allied military control was to be in the hands of an inter-Allied commission, which in turn was to be advised by John F. Stevens, head of the Russian Railway Service corps, and a Technical Board.

President Wilson regarded the railway plan as of "inestimable value to the people of Russia and the United States, as well as the world in general . . . thereby giving practical effect to the principle of the open door." Advising Congress of American policy in reference to the Trans-Siberian and Chinese Eastern Railways, Wilson wrote:

It is felt that this matter can be treated entirely apart from the general Russian problem, as, irrespective of what our policy may be toward Russia, and irrespective of further (future) Russian developments, it is essential that we maintain the policy of the open door with reference to the Siberian and particularly the Chinese Eastern Railway.

The Inter-Allied Railway Agreement changed completely the character of intervention in Siberia. The primary concern of American military forces now became the restoration and protection of the railways instead of the rescue of the Czechs. The latter were now participating in the execution of the railway plan. In effect, the improvement of the transportation system served to aid the anti-Bolshevik cause. Thus, despite its denials, the United States became an active participant in the Russian Civil War. President Wilson justified this course on the grounds of maintaining the open door in Siberia and North Manchuria and preserving Russia's territorial integrity. In this respect the conclusion of the Railway Agreement represented a victory for the United States and the liberal civilian elements in the Japanese government.

The Japanese military were not slow in revealing their real attitude toward cooperation with the United States in Siberia. Despite the Railway Agreement and continuous efforts to avoid factional strife, American forces were constantly embroiled in difficulty with Japan or with the Siberian factions which she supported. At times incidents with both almost led to actual hostilities.

The Kolchak or Omsk government, established in November 1918, was supreme in Western Siberia. Supported by the Czechs, it maintained an army which was engaged in conducting a campaign against the Bolsheviks. Kolchak was supported strongly by the British and French representatives in Siberia, who were eager to have the Allied governments recognize his rule. Kolchak, however, was unable to control two independent Cossack leaders, Gregorii Semenov and Ivan Kalmykov, who used the chaotic conditions in Siberia as a means of increasing their own wealth and power. Senemov destroyed railway transportation, interrupted telegraphic communications, and terrorized the eastern regions with his irresponsible actions. There was ample evidence to indicate that his activities were directly encouraged and supported by Japan. Japanese military authorities refused to protect the representatives of the Technical Board in the performance of their railway duties, despite Semenov's hostile acts against them. They maintained that such actions would be interference in Russian internal affairs.

To Roland S. Morris, American ambassador to Japan, the Japanese plan was perfectly clear:

Baffled by the railway agreement in their organized attempt to take possession of the Chinese Eastern and Trans-Siberian Railway as far as Chita and thus dominate eastern Siberia and northern Manchuria the Japanese Government is countenancing a less obvious, but a more insidious scheme of operating through the Cossack organization which is the only substantial support Kolchak has east of Chita. It will not be difficult for Japan to dispose of the eastern Cossacks when they have served the purpose.

While the Omsk authorities were disturbed about the actions of the Japanese and Cossacks, they were equally provoked with the "un-neutral" policy of American troops. General William S. Graves, commander of American expeditionary forces, held rigidly to a strict interpretation of his instructions and refused to take action for or against either Kolchak or the Bolsheviks, except insofar as each side might benefit from the protection of the railway sectors and military stores assigned to his command. The Omsk government stated flatly that American troops were accomplishing no useful purpose in Siberia but were doing actual harm in tending to prolong disturbed conditions. The British and French governments sustained the objections of the Omsk government.

President Wilson was obviously troubled about the entire Siberian situation. He presented his problem to the Council of Four in Paris. He pointed out that although the United States did not believe in Kolchak, the British and French military representatives in Siberia were supporting him. Kolchak, who regarded American soldiers as neutrals, was quite irritated by their presence on the railway. The Cossacks were also antagonistic toward American soldiers. Wilson suspected that the Japanese would be glad to see a collision between the two groups. In these circumstances, Wilson believed that the United States must either take sides with Kolchak and send a much stronger force to Siberia or withdraw. If the United States aided Kolchak and increased its forces in Siberia, Japan

would increase hers still more. If American troops continued merely to guard the railroad and to maintain a neutral position, Wilson was advised that collisions would occur, which might result in actual war. If American troops were withdrawn, Siberia would be left to the Japanese and Kolchak. The President's dilemma was quite evident. Although he favored a neutral policy toward Russia and Siberia, at the same time he did not wish to withdraw American soldiers from Siberia and leave Japan in control of the situation. This would mean an end to the cherished open door policy.

Personally, Wilson had always believed that the proper policy for the Allied and Associated powers was "to clear out of Russia and leave it to the Russians to fight it out among themselves." Yet for two reasons American troops continued to remain in Siberia. For all practical purposes American evacuation would have left Japan in virtual control of North Manchuria and Eastern Siberia. Moreover, Britain, France, and Japan were opposed to withdrawal. President Wilson did not wish to jeopardize his program at the Peace Conference by independent action. Thus, in order to block Japan and to further his League, Wilson followed a policy which appeared to be totally at variance not only with the principles which he had enunciated concerning Russia, but also with the principles of his proposed League. As time went on, these clashes between what Wilson said and what he did made the American position in Siberia even more difficult. Wilson soon found it impossible to keep American troops in Siberia without actively aiding Kolchak. Whatever may be said concerning America's neutrality in Siberia in 1918, there is little doubt that in 1919 the State Department actively supported and aided

Kolchak despite the fact that Wilson himself admitted that the American people did not believe in Kolchak. However, the Bolsheviks themselves conceded America's justification in following such a policy, when in 1933, after being shown certain documents concerning America's policy, they agreed to drop all claims against America for her part in the Siberian intervention. As Cordell Hull pointed out, "These latter documents made clear to Litvinov that American forces had not been in Siberia to wrest territory from Russia, but to ensure the withdrawal of the Japanese, who had a far larger force in Siberia with the intent to occupy it permanently."

It would seem to be notable, however, that throughout the intervention the American public was permitted to believe that the United States went into Siberia to combat Bolshevism. It was difficult for the State Department to refute this belief while the United States was at war. Japan was an ally, and it was not considered diplomatic to question publicly the motives of one's allies, especially when a fear existed that Japan might possibly join the Central Powers. Even after the war was over, the popular feeling persisted that intervention was solely to defeat the Bolsheviks. This sentiment was intensified by the actions of the underlings in the State Department who assumed control of America's policy in Siberia upon Wilson's illness, and who themselves favored Kolchak and wanted him to receive the greatest aid possible.

Since the attitude of the State Department had long since ceased to be neutral, why did the United States withdraw its troops in 1920? Why were they not maintained and reinforced? The answer appears in a simple note written by Secretary Lansing to the President:

The truth of the matter is the simple fact that the Kolchak Government has utterly collapsed; the armies of the Bolsheviki have advanced into Eastern Siberia, where they are reported to be acting with moderation. The people seem to prefer them to the officers of the Kolchak regime. Further, the Bolshevik army is approaching the region where our soldiers are, and contact with them will lead to open hostilities and to many complications. In other words, if we do not withdraw we shall have to wage war against the Bolsheviki.

American troops remained in Vladivostok until a substantial portion of the Czech troops were afloat. The last contingent of Americans left Vladivostok on April 1, 1920. Few tears were shed over their departure. America's part in the Siberian situation had already been summarized aptly, if somewhat facetiously, by the remark that "some might have liked us more if we had intervened less. . . . some might have disliked us less if we had intervened more," but that having intervened "no more nor no less than we actually did, nobody had any use for us at all."

Christopher Lasch: AMERICAN INTERVENTION:
A DELUDED EFFORT

Professor Christopher Lasch, specialist in American social history, is currently teaching at Northwestern University. The article presented below grows out of an earlier study entitled American Liberals and the Russian Revolution. *In it, he contends that American intervention in Siberia was based on the illusion that the Bolsheviks were actually German agents.*

THE participation of the United States in the Allied Expedition to Siberia in 1918 remains a baffling episode, in spite of all that has been written about it. What were American troops doing fighting on the side of the counter-revolution in Russia? How could Americans reconcile intervention with "self-determination"? The question haunts all studies of the subject. Indeed, the need to excuse has taken precedence over the need to understand. As a result, we are hardly nearer to understanding than we were in 1918.

It is not easy even to excuse intervention. Efforts to do so encounter at once two difficult facts. In the first place, the United States did not go into Russia at once — in March, 1918, when the Allies wanted to. Instead it waited until August. Why? Wilson's hesitation seems to confirm the suspicion that intervention was a nasty business from start to finish. If it wasn't, why did he wait so long before acting, and why, when he did act, did he act with such obvious reluctance? As the *Nation* put it at the time:

From the start the unfriendly intent behind Allied intervention in Russia was revealed by the frank though futile opposition of President Wilson. His objections gave the situation away; he admitted it to be a bad business before he became a partner in it, and his final surrender served only to emphasize the helplessness of benevolent intentions before the cynical determination of the controlling forces among the Allies.

In the second place, the official reason given for intervention was never very convincing. The British and the French talked of restoring the eastern front, and although the method proposed seemed somewhat fantastic, the desirability of doing so, in the face of the great German drive in the west in the spring of 1918, was beyond question. But the United States government never accepted the second-front theory of intervention. It justified the sending of American troops to Siberia solely as a means of relieving the Czech Legion, which had become involved in hostilities with the Bolsheviks in its effort to get out of Russia by way of Vladivostok. But that explanation, while it might have been plausible in May, 1918, was not very plausible in August, when it was put forward as the official policy governing intervention, because by that time the Czechs were moving westward over the Trans-Siberian Railway in an effort to reunite their scattered force. The government itself, in its statement of August 4, 1918, referred to

From Christopher Lasch, "American Intervention in Siberia: A Reinterpretation," *Political Science Quarterly*, LXXVII, No. 2 (June, 1962), pp. 205–223. Reprinted by permission of the Academy of Political Science.

the "westward-moving Czecho-Slovaks." Critics of intervention immediately seized on the phrase as proof, if further proof were needed, that the government of the United States had openly thrown its influence on the side of the counter-revolution.

It was not until after the Second World War that students of the subject worked out an answer to these questions. Then the answer seemed so obvious that it was hard to see why no one had thought of it before. The answer was simply that the real reason for intervention had never been avowed; it *couldn't* be avowed at the time, not publicly at any rate, because to have done so would have embarrassed an ally. That explained why aid to the Czechs had never seemed a satisfactory explanation; it also explained Wilson's hesitation. Wilson hesitated because he was not sure whether the Japanese, who saw in Russia's internal troubles a chance to lop off Siberia, would be so bold as to land troops in Russia in the face of American opposition. For a time, it looked as if the United States could prevent Japanese intervention simply by making it clear that the United States could not approve such a step. But as the summer wore on, it became clear that the Japanese intended to act anyway. Only then did Wilson acquiesce in the plan to send a joint Japanese-American expedition into Siberia. That was better, in the last analysis, than unilateral Japanese action. By joining Japan, the United States might restrain her almost as effectively, in fact, as if she had been free to oppose her outright. Outright opposition, of course, was impossible because Japan was unfortunately an "Associated Power."

Such was the explanation which at last seemed to acquit the United States of the crime of having taken part in the counter-revolution. It was no coincidence that it first emerged in the late 1940's. We had just fought a devastating war with Japan. Naturally historians tended to read back our antipathy to Japan into the diplomacy of the First World War. Nor is it surprising that the theory that intervention was designed to stop Japan continued to flourish in the 1950's. The demands of the Cold War required us to show that we were not the aggressors in that conflict — the origins of which were now also projected back to 1918. It had never been our intention to interfere with the revolution in Russia. As long as it confined itself to Russia we had had only sympathy for the revolution. We intervened only to save the Russians from the Japanese. If anything, the Russians should have been grateful for our help.

The anti-Japanese theory of intervention, first formulated by John Albert White in 1950 and repeated after him by all who sought to justify intervention, thus accorded well with the exigencies of the moment. It was clear, it was simple, it explained everything that needed to be explained. It had everything to commend it except accuracy. For in fact it rested on a fundamental confusion between American policy toward Japan after 1919, which was one of hostility, and American policy toward Japan during the First World War, which was almost unmarred by suspicion or bad feeling. The anti-Japanese theory of intervention, in other words, was purely retrospective. Having served its propagandistic purpose, it can now be discarded.

The difficulty is to find something to take its place. Those who are unhappy with it — William Appleman Williams, for example — fall back on the original anti-interventionist argument that intervention was really designed to overthrow the Bolshevik regime. But that argument is itself open to grave objections. It requires us to believe that Wilson knew exactly what he was doing, when there is every evidence that he and most of his contemporaries were uncertain and confused. It requires us to believe that he and his advisers hated Bolshevism because it was a threat to capitalism, when a thorough study of American opinion on the revolution shows that most Americans, including Wilson himself, were not greatly disturbed by the economic theories of the Bolsheviks. It requires us to believe, in short, that American policy was determined in strict accordance with the interests of the business community. It is therefore open to all the objections to which a crude economic interpretation of history is usually open. Historians might well take refuge in the Japanese theory of intervention if only because the economic interpretation is on its merits so unconvincing.

It is the purpose of this discussion to show that *both* theories are erroneous and to suggest a third theory which will explain what neither one of them does explain.

II

The best argument against the Japanese theory is simply that nobody at the time the decision was under consideration cited fear of what Japan would do in Siberia as a reason for joining the proposed expedition. Only after the decision had been made, and after the war with Germany had ended, did the fear of Japan come to influence American policy toward Russia. At the time — that is, in the spring and summer of 1918 — fear of Japan was cited as a reason for *not* intervening, if it was cited at all. Those who wanted to intervene argued, on the other hand, that the Japanese had only the best intentions in the world. They were impatient with those who argued that Japan could not be trusted.

Thus one finds that the ambassador to Russia, a convert to intervention in the summer of 1918 (he had opposed it in March), saw the problem as one of *inducing* Japan to join the expedition. He seemed quite unaware that Japan was one of its instigators. "In my judgment," he wrote to Lansing, "no promises should be exacted of Japan and no promises made to her if she will consent to intervene without them. If Japan can be induced to join with us in intervention we need have no fear concerning her exactions or demands when the war ends." He added that in any case, the Allies would "dominate the peace table" and that Japan would "be compelled to accept the just terms offered whether she likes them or not."

These views were shared by the State Department. Frank Polk tried to convince Lansing of the "squareness of the Japanese in [the] Siberian matter." But Lansing did not need to be convinced. In July, 1919, long after many Americans *had* developed qualms about the Japanese, Lansing wrote in his diary:

Japanese designs as to Siberia are worrying a lot of Americans, who see in everything that the Japanese Government do some hidden motive, some insidious purpose. The present anxiety is caused by the large number of Japanese troops now in Siberia, from which it is deduced that Japan intends to annex Eastern Siberia or at least obtain all the valuable concessions of that region by bargain or threat.

The Japanese are not fools. They know that a white race would never submit to the domination of a yellow race. [!] To take the sovereignty or economic control of Eastern Siberia would mean endless trouble for Japan, as the Siberians would never rest until they had driven the Japanese out of the country.

I have little patience with these people

who are forever on the verge of hysterics about the deep and wicked schemes of Japan.

To be sure, Lansing himself, though hardly on the "verge of hysterics," had at an earlier stage in the sequence of events shared some of these misgivings about Japan. In the last week of July, 1918, after the decision to intervene had finally been taken (but only afterwards), relations between the United States and Japan were strained by the desire of the Japanese to send in more troops than had originally been agreed upon. But what the administration feared "at heart," as Frank Polk put it, was not a preponderance of Japanese troops as such but the "impression which would be made on the Russian mind." Polk, speaking for the State Department, was quite prepared to recognize the "special position of Japan" in East Asia; indeed he considered that the United States had already done so in the Lansing-Ishii agreement of 1917, and to do so again, as the Japanese were asking, appeared unnecessary. That at least is what Polk told the Japanese ambassador. Perhaps he was only being tactful. But Lansing, Wilson and Colonel House had all said the same thing in private, on any number of occasions.

The great fear in Washington was that Japanese intervention "would be received with genuine disfavor [by the Russians] and would probably be met by armed resistance." Russia would then turn to Germany for help and "might definitely ally herself with the Central Powers." So felt Lansing, and so the President himself. "With the foregoing," Lansing noted, "the President entirely agrees." Somewhat later Sir William Wiseman, special British agent in the United States, wrote after an interview with Wilson that Wilson's objection to intervention was "simply that such action on the part of the

Allies would play into German hands." In another interview with Wiseman, Wilson was more explicit. "If we relied mainly on Japanese military assistance we should rally the Russians against us, excepting for a small reactionary body who would join anybody to destroy the Bolsheviks." When Wiseman objected that "it was not possible to make the situation worse than it was now," Wilson said that:

that was where he entirely disagreed. We could make it much worse by putting the Germans in a position where they could organize Russia in a national movement against Japan. If that was done he would not be surprised to see Russian soldiers fighting with the Germans on the Western Front.

So far was the President from giving the impression of suspecting the motives of the Japanese, however, that the British in their impatience began almost to believe, as Wiseman wrote to Lord Reading, "that there must be some secret understanding between the U. S. and Japan, of which [the other Allies] were not aware" — some understanding, that is, according to which the Americans and the Japanese would divide a Siberian sphere of influence between them.

As for Colonel House, not the fear of Japan but solicitude for the "Russian mind" was the burden of his misgivings about intervention from start to finish. Nor were these opinions peculiarly his own; they were shared, he said, even by so conservative a statesman as Elihu Root.

He agrees with you and with me [House wrote to Wilson at one point] as to the danger of the proposed Japanese intervention in Siberia. He thinks that even if Japan should announce her purpose to retire when the war was over, or at the mandate of the peace conference, the racial dislike which the Russians have for the Japanese would throw Russia into the arms of Germany.

When the Japanese in violation of their understanding with the United States dispatched additional troops to Siberia, the United States not only protested that such action would antagonize the loyal Russians but threatened to withdraw from the whole undertaking if Japan and the other Allies were bent on "a large expedition." This curious threat was reiterated as late as September, 1918, when the expedition was well under way. If our aim was to contain the Japanese in Siberia, a more logical policy, it would seem, would have been to send additional troops to the area, for to retire would merely have given the Japanese a free hand. To be sure, there were not many troops that could have been spared from the western front; and the talk of withdrawal may have been in any case only a bluff. But it seems reasonable to conclude that what disturbed the State Department at this point was not Japanese expansion as such, but the repercussions in Russian politics of an expedition almost exclusively Japanese in character — its effect on the "Russian mind." If the "loyal" Russians, who presumably hated Japan as much as they hated the Germans and the Bolsheviks, were to object, then the United States might retain their good will by dissociating itself from an unpopular policy. From that point of view withdrawal made some sense.

These doubts, then, about how Japanese intervention would strike the Russians explain the administration's hesitation and indecision during the long debate over intervention in the spring and summer of 1918. But it should be noted that those who worried about the effect of intervention on the course of events in Russia had already decided, quite independently of the Japanese, that *some* intervention was desirable. As soon as the Bolsheviks signed the Treaty of Brest Litovsk, the administration began to speculate about how Russia could be saved from "German domination" — and this fear of German domination and/or a Russo-German alliance was the central consideration in the deliberations which followed. The question was just how Russia could be "saved." There were two alternatives: a program of economic aid designed to get Russia back on its feet so that the Russians would not become dependent on Germany, and military intervention, designed to oust the Germans by force. (Some people, in addition, thought of actually restoring a second front, but as we have noted, that idea never carried much weight in the United States. The military men condemned it as utterly impracticable.)

Both alternatives were beset with difficulties. If economic aid were sent, through what forces in Russia could it be distributed? The Bolsheviks would use Allied aid as a means of defeating their enemies, and vice versa. How could economic aid be kept out of Russian politics?

Military action raised a different problem, but one equally formidable. Which of the Allies could afford to send a force into Russia? The troops of Great Britain, France and the United States were tied up on the western front. "The only country that can send a formidable army into Russia at this time," as Ambassador Francis wrote, "is Japan, against which there is a strong prejudice among the Russians who fear that Japan may have a covetous eye upon Siberia." Japanese intervention might therefore provoke exactly what it was designed to prevent, a Russo-German rapprochement.

It was in these terms that the problem presented itself to the administration.

Note that in none of these discussions was the problem presented as a matter of intervening in order to prevent the Japanese from gobbling up Siberia. It was the *Germans,* not the Japanese, who were presumed to be on the verge of gobbling it up. The only question was whether the Russians would see the matter in the same light as the Allies saw. By July, the administration believed that it had brought the Russians around to the Allied view of things. No sooner was that accomplished, however, than the Japanese proposed sending in extra troops. The administration then objected because, as Polk told the Japanese ambassador, it would frighten the Russians into the arms of Germany. His statement, in the light of the rest of the evidence, has to be taken on its merits. He meant exactly what he said.

There were many Americans, of course, who insisted that Japan could not be trusted at all. The Secretary of War, Newton D. Baker, held that opinion, and so did Wilson himself, at bottom. But Baker opposed intervention all along, precisely because he *was* afraid of Japan. Thus he advised Wilson in November, 1918, that "the presence of our troops in Siberia is being used by the Japanese [sic] as a cloak for their own presence and operations there. . . ." He did note that some people were now arguing that the presence of the Japanese in Siberia had become a reason for American troops to remain. (That, he said, was one of two reasons given for remaining, the other being "that we must have a military force to act as guardians and police for any civil relief effort we are able to direct toward Siberia.") But the presence of the Japanese seemed to him a good reason for getting out. "The longer we stay, the more Japaneze there are and the more difficult it will be to induce Japan to

withdraw her forces. . . ." Wilson himself appears to have agreed with Baker on this point. David Hunter Miller quotes him as saying in January, 1919, that:

he did not trust the Japanese; *that he had trusted them before* [my italics], — in fact they had broken their agreement about Siberia. We had sent 7,000 troops to Siberia and they promised to send about the same number but had sent 70,000 and had occupied all the strategic points as far as Irkutsk, and that he would not trust them again.

His distrust of the Japanese, however, merely reinforced the President's determination to bring the whole business of intervention to an end.

But as Wilson soon discovered, it was "harder to get out than it was to go in." The problem was how to get out without leaving Russia in a complete shambles, torn by civil war and threatened in the west by a resurgent Germany and in the east by Japan. The war having ended, it was now possible for Wilson to see the situation in the Far East in particular in a clearer light — to see it in the light in which historians have insisted he saw it all along. Until November, 1917, the minds of American officials had been riveted to the problem of defeating Germany, and they weighed every international development as it bore on that single objective. Japanese intervention was objectionable because it might throw Russia into the arms of Germany. By the time the peace conference assembled, however, that danger seemed for the moment at least to have subsided. What now became clear was that Japanese intervention was undesirable in itself. The mirage of Japanese good intentions quickly dissolved. At the peace conference the Japanese design of a "new order" in east Asia (although it was not yet called that) for the first time became unmistakable. Japan's determination to get recognition for the special concessions which she had wrung from China brought her into direct conflict with President Wilson, for the arrangement she proposed violated not only the principle of self-determination but the cherished (although for some time almost forgotten) Open Door. By May, 1919, Wilson was sufficiently alarmed about the Japanese penetration of Siberia to give it as a reason for supporting Admiral Kolchak.

But these later fears about Japan must not be read back into the period in which the decision to intervene was taken. During that earlier period the Wilson administration had great confidence in the good faith of the Japanese, who were allies in the war against Germany. This confidence may have been misplaced and decisions based on it mistakes, but the mistakes were discovered only in retrospect. That probably accounts for our feeling, in the 1920's and '30's, that the Japanese had actively betrayed our friendship. In the same way we felt betrayed, after another war with Germany, by our friends and allies the Russians.

III

One theory of intervention insists that it was directed against the Japanese. The other theory insists that it was really directed against the Bolsheviks. But the evidence already cited seems to indicate that intervention was directed against neither, but against the Germans. As a matter of fact, that is how the administration explained intervention to the American people: the Czecho-Slovaks were engaged in heroic resistance to the Germans and had to be rescued. (That was the unmistakable implication of the explanatory statement issued by the State Department, although the Germans were

not mentioned by name. Neither were the Bolsheviks nor their opponents in Russia, with whom the Czechs were cooperating.) It is difficult sometimes for historians to accept what people say at its face value. It is particularly difficult when what people say doesn't make much sense, as was the case in 1918. But that fact — the nonsensical nature of the discussion regarding intervention — is precisely the most important thing about the whole episode.

We can better understand why the United States finally joined the expedition to Siberia if we remember that one consideration took precedence over all others in arriving at such a decision. If military intervention was to be undertaken, it had to be reconciled with Russia's right to "self-determination," so dear to American liberals. But we must not think of the explanation which eventually emerged, and which served to reconcile the contradiction, as merely a rationalization. We must not assume, in other words, that the decision was taken for some other reason which could not publicly be avowed, after which a plausible excuse was invented. The excuse and the reason for intervention were one and the same thing. When the administration said that it was sending aid to the Czechs, it meant exactly that and no more.

But hadn't the Czechs become participants in the Russian civil war? Weren't they fighting the Bolsheviks? On the contrary, advocates of intervention insisted that they were fighting not the Bolsheviks but the *Germans.* How could the Czechs in Siberia be fighting the Germans, whose armies were thousands of miles away? There were two reasons for thinking that they were. In the first place, it was widely believed in the United States that the Bolsheviks at Germany's bidding had provided arms to the German prisoners of war, captured by the armies of the Tsar and the Provisional Government, who were scattered all over Russia and Siberia. That these prisoners were so numerous and so highly organized as to constitute an army capable of taking over all Siberia, and that they were armed to the teeth, were illusions nourished by the American wartime habit of exaggerating the prowess of the enemy. In fact, most of the prisoners were not German at all, but Austrian; and, although they numbered altogether about a million, they were in no sense an army. At most only a few thousand of them were armed. Two Allied investigators sent out in March, 1918, found large numbers of armed prisoners only at Omsk, and even there they found less than a thousand. Thomas Masaryk, commander of the Czech Legion, who could hardly be accused of Bolshevik sympathies, later testified: "Nowhere in Siberia, between March 15th and April 2nd, did I see armed German and Austrian prisoners."

Nevertheless, Americans were convinced that all Siberia was about to fall into German hands. Even Lansing, who has been pictured by his admirers and by his detractors alike as a hard-headed anti-Bolshevik, a man who advocated intervention, not only in order to help the Czechs, but as a means of getting rid of Lenin and Trotsky — even Lansing came to favor intervention only when he was convinced that the Germans were about to overrun Siberia. Thus on March 18 he opposed a Japanese landing on the grounds that it would antagonize the Russian people, but four days later, after hearing alarming reports of German advances eastward — occupation by German troops of points as far east as Irkutsk now seemed not impossible — he changed his mind. "The restoration of order in Siberia when the confusion is due to civil strife between Russian factions" was in his opinion inadmissible, but "the wresting of control of the territory from an organized body of troops operating under German officers" was another matter. When, after the Czech uprising (May, 1918), Lansing finally became convinced of the necessity for intervention, he put the question to himself in the following terms: "Furnishing protection and assistance to the Czecho-Slovaks, who are so loyal to our cause, is a very different thing from sending an army into Siberia to restore order and to save the Russians from themselves." The United States, he thought, should "cooperate with [the Czechs] in disarming and dispersing the Germans and Austrians [sic] who oppose them."

The reports of Ambassador Francis in Russia probably had something to do with converting the Secretary of State to this view of things. As early as May, 1918, Francis cabled that the Germans dominated the Soviet government and that the German ambassador "was practically dictator in Moscow." By the end of that month he was "almost convinced that Lenin and possibly Trotsky are pliable tools if not responsive German agents." Intervention, therefore, was to be regarded as simply another battle in the struggle with German autocracy.

Occasionally someone admitted, as William Howard Taft wrote a few days after the first Allied landings at Vladivostok, that "we are now at war with the Bolsheviki." But most people maintained the fiction that the Bolsheviks were not involved. Even if they were involved, however, that did not necessarily mean that the United States had cast its lot on the side of the counter-revolution, as opponents of intervention maintained. The Bolsheviks, when one thought about it, were not really revolutionists at all. They were German agents. That was the second reason, and the most important reason, for thinking that the Czechs (and therefore the Allies) were fighting only the armies of the Kaiser. Bolshevism itself was merely an extension of Kaiserism.

The need to believe that proposition accounts for the intense interest, in the United States, in the so-called Sisson documents, which purported to prove that the Bolsheviks were hired agents of Germany. No other Allied country gave these documents the attention which they attracted in the United States. Only in the United States were they endorsed and published by the government, the President himself professing, in the face of abundant evidence to the contrary, to be "thoroughly satisfied" of their authenticity. Only in the United States was their authenticity vouched for by eminent historians and accepted without question by most of the press. In Europe, on the other hand, they were treated by governments and peoples alike with suspicion and scorn. Such an attitude on the part of the Old World reflected, not a nicer sense of propriety, but merely the fact that the British and the French advocated intervention frankly as a means of overthrowing the Bolsheviks (as well as of restoring an eastern front). Only those who were committed to the view that intervention was directed solely at Germany and thus did not constitute intervention in Russia's internal affairs needed the Sisson documents to buttress their case. Those who had no qualms about intervening in order to overthrow a regime which was undesirable in itself, regardless of its alleged connections with Germany, did not have to prove the existence of a German-Bolshevik conspiracy. Lansing, for instance, refused to have anything to do with the Sisson documents, because, once he had finally taken the step of accepting intervention as a necessity, he was not averse to using it on behalf of the counter-revolution. It was no coincidence that it was the conservative State Department that opposed publication of the Sisson documents, while Wilson and George Creel, without consulting the State Department, pushed them on the public in order to explain the disparity between the principle of self-determination and the fact of intervention.

IV

It was not easy for those who opposed intervention to understand that the administration thought of the expedition to Siberia as merely another way of defeating the great enemy, Germany. Remembering the way in which European monarchists had intervened in the French revolution, they assumed that intervention in Russia was prompted only by a desire to overthrow the Bolshevik regime. Predisposed toward an economic interpretation of history, they suspected that intervention was an imperialistic conspiracy directed against a promising experiment in social democracy, a conspiracy of international bankers to restore the old regime with which they had enjoyed such profitable business relations.

The whole of this Russian situation [one liberal wrote] can be traced down to this — . . . the French government soaked many millions in Russian bonds years ago. . . . At that time the Russian socialists protested and said they would never pay those debts if they overthrew the czar. And they overthrew the czar and told the French they didn't intend to pay those debts. So the French want to oust the bolsheviki. And they have been behind a lot of the propaganda against them. Many other elements enter of course — the instinctive fear of socialism which so many people have helps. And England as well as the United States has money in the old government or the Kerensky government.

Intervention, in short, was "class war."

Historians who deplore intervention follow the contemporary liberal critics in regarding it as an attempt to restore the old regime, or at least to restore some regime with which Western capitalists could do business. In such a view, the publication of the Sisson documents can be explained only as a deliberate effort to create a "red scare" by associating Bolshevism with the German menace. But there is no more evidence to sustain such a theory than there is evidence to sustain the theory that intervention was directed against Japan — a theory which critics of intervention have always rightly rejected.

The facts of the matter are more depressing than the critics ever imagined. It was possible, after all, to make out a case for massive intervention against the Bolsheviks on the grounds of self-interest. Winston Churchill stated such a case before the Versailles conference, before he was quickly overruled by Wilson and Lloyd George. For Churchill, the real objection to intervention was not that it was undertaken in the first place, but that it was undertaken half-heartedly; and there is a good deal to be said for his argument. Whether a massive assault would have worked is another matter, but such a proposal could be defended. What could not possibly be defended was what was actually done — sending in an army to meet an imaginary enemy. Intervention made sense, as the administration conceived of it, only if one assumed that the Bolsheviks were German agents and that they had given arms to the German and Austrian prisoners of war so that the Central Empires could take over Siberia. None of these things happened to be true.

The whole business rested on an illusion of staggering proportions.

If it seems preposterous that men in their right minds could have entertained such an illusion, the answer is that Wilson and most of his countrymen were not perhaps *in* their right minds. They were at war, and war has a way of distorting one's view of the world. That seems particularly to be true of the United States. For Americans in 1918, there was only one enemy, Germany — an enemy so subtle, so insidious, so relentless in its determination to conquer the world that it had launched revolutionary movements to subvert free institutions wherever they existed. These movements, of which the Russian revolution was the most terrifying example, were of course not revolutionary at all, but secretly allied with the reactionary designs of imperial Germany. Nor were they in any sense spontaneous; on the contrary, they were planned, directed and financed by Germany herself. They could be put down, in the long run, only by force.

These views are so manifestly absurd that historians for a long time have simply ignored their existence. But perhaps it will be easier to accept their existence as a fact and to judge the hold they exercised over the men of that time, if we consider that Americans now entertain exactly the same views about the Soviet Union. Thus, in our own time the revolutionary movements in such countries as Cuba, Egypt and Indonesia are regarded by Americans as having been conceived and dominated by Russia. Our policy has been based on that assumption, just as our policy was based on a similar assumption in 1918.

William Appleman Williams: AMERICAN INTERVENTION: STRICTLY ANTI-BOLSHEVIK

William Appleman Williams, a specialist in American foreign relations and social change, is currently on the faculty of Oregon State University. In addition to many articles and pamphlets he has published several major works in American diplomatic history. The selection below is a revision and expansion of the earlier research he did on American intervention in Russia first appearing in his American-Russian Relations, 1781–1947.

THE VIGOROUS reassertion in February 1918 of the fundamentally anti-Bolshevik attitudes of American leaders placed President Wilson under increasing pressure from the logic of his own outlook to intervene directly in Russia. His problem henceforward was to find a way to act against the Bolsheviks that would enable him to resolve or rationalize his moral dilemma, that would be effective against the revolutionary forces and that would offer a way of preventing Japan from exploiting intervention to weaken or even subvert the Open Door Policy in Asia.

It is not surprising, therefore, that Wilson and Lansing slapped aside a serious and dramatic French proposal to try collaboration with the Bolsheviks, or that they did so in an instantaneous and ruthless refusal. This strking reversal of earlier French policy, which favored military intervention, evolved in response to the clear indications that the Bolsheviks needed and wanted Allied assistance against the Germans. Renewed German operations in northern Russia prompted Trotsky to advise the coalition or revolutionaries in Murmansk on March 1 and 2, 1918, that it was "obliged to accept any help from the Allied Missions." Lenin

supported that decision and later issued general orders to resist the Germans.

American and French representatives in Moscow knew of these decisions, and interpreted them as verification of their own estimates of Bolshevik policies. The American military advisors, who had been seeing Trotsky almost as often as Robins, filed strong recommendations in favor of supporting the Bolshevik effort against the Germans. Coupled with his continuing evaluation of the nature and meaning of the Revolution per se, this convergence of events led the French military attaché, Jacques Sadoul, to extend even further his own talents and energy in an effort to convince his superiors in Russia and Paris that cooperation was both the most rational and the most promising policy for France to follow.

Combining strong emotion and powerful logic with persuasive language, Sadoul's argument momentarily carried the day. The French Government reconsidered its heretofore militant anti-Bolshevism, supported Sadoul's negotiations with the Bolsheviks, and formally asked the United States if it would join in general collaboration with Lenin and Trotsky. American leaders considered the French proposal on February 19, con-

From William A. Williams, "American Intervention in Russia, 1917–1920" (Part Two), *Studies on the Left*, IV (Winter 1964), pp. 39–57. Reprinted by permission of the author.

ducting their talks in the context of a militantly anti-Bolshevik memorandum prepared by Miles.

The United States, Miles argued, defined democracy in terms of "the political freedom of its people." On the other hand, the Bolsheviks held that democracy was based on "equal economic freedom." His conclusion was unequivocal. "Fundamentally, these two conceptions are as different as black from white. It is idle to attempt to reconcile them as so many do. They are wholly different and cannot be reconciled." The Bolshevik view was "revolutionary in the deepest sense," and its advocates "have hitherto lived in the shadow." It is apparent, and should be made explicit, that American leaders were every bit as inflexible and deterministic as they accused the Bolsheviks of being; and, further, that it was the Bolsheviks who proved to be the more willing to diverge from the dictates of their theoretical and general opposition to collaboration with capitalist nations.

The decision on the French proposal was wholly in keeping with the logic and tone of the memorandum by Miles. He had not, of course, changed anybody's mind. But his analysis did reinforce the existing anti-Bolshevik consensus. Lansing personally took the French request to President Wilson. His brief pencilled notation documents their attitude: "This is out of the question. Submitted to Pres't who says the same thing." American leaders were of course interested in re-establishing resistance to the Germans on the eastern front, but they were not sufficiently anti-German to overcome their anti-Bolshevism.

Robins had no direct knowledge of this mid-February decision, and his efforts to arrange such cooperation with the Bolsheviks came to a climax between February 22, when the Bolshevik Central Committee voted to accept aid from the allies (with Lenin casting the crucial vote), and March 5, when Trotsky and Lenin gave Robins a written and specific inquiry designed to initiate a serious discussion concerning aid from the United States.

There is some evidence that a full copy of this document failed to reach Washington until after the Bolsheviks ratified the Brest-Litovsk treaty of peace with Germany. Even if this is true, and the evidence is not wholly convincing, the delay is far less significant than such writers as George Frost Kennan have made it appear. *Top American leaders already had explicit knowledge of the Bolshevik interest in obtaining assistance from the United States.* Furthermore, and as Washington was advised by several American military representatives in Russia, ratification of the treaty with Germany did not prevent the Germans from reopening their offensive — or the Bolsheviks from opposing that new attack as best they could. As late as March 26, for example, Francis told Lansing that the Red Army "is the only hope for saving European Russia from Germany." American policy-makers *could* have responded favorably to the overture from Lenin and Trotsky whenever it actually did arrive. For that matter, they could have offered such negotiations on their own initiative. They did neither.

Wilson's message to the Congress of Soviets of March 10 made it clear beyond any question that he had no intention even of exploring the possibilities of such cooperation. He bluntly told the Russian people that the United States, despite its great sympathy for their travail, was not going to help them through the Bolshevik Government. His words further carried the strong implication that the Bolsheviks were in league with the Germans. This document was prepared, moreover, in the course of continuing discussions designed to evolve a plan of intervention which would resolve the moral and practical dilemmas confronting Wilson and other American leaders. By February 26, for example, Lansing was referring in his conversations with Wilson to "our proposed policy." The resulting decision seems to have been produced by several convergent pressures, and was based upon a rather subtle strategy for controlling the variables involved in intervention.

After their proposal to collaborate with the Bolsheviks had been dismissed out of hand, the French returned to nagging Wilson for some kind of intervention in Siberia. The British supported this campaign to break down the President's resistance. And the Japanese, of course, continued their own push for permission to move onto the mainland of Asia. These pressures on the United States were powerful in and of themselves, and gained additional strength from the political and psychological circumstances. Wilson was opposing other Allied suggestions, for example, and he seems to have felt that he might gain some political ground by agreeing to some form of intervention. The psychological factor involved the fatigue which was apparent in Wilson and Lansing. They were tired men, and were no doubt particularly weary of the Russian issue. The inclination to go on in and be done with it may have become quite strong once they had turned their backs on the idea of working with or through the Bolsheviks.

Even so, there was more than political higgling and ennui involved in Wilson's decision in February to approve Japanese intervention. For one thing, Lansing and Wilson seem to have concluded that

Japan might do something regardless of American or allied approval. "My own belief," Lansing fretted in a letter to the President on February 27, "is that Japan intends to go into Siberia anyway." This raised the very difficult question of how to limit and control the Japanese. Lansing first encouraged the Chinese to hold the line in Manchuria. He told them that the United States wanted "the Chinese Government to take over and guard that part of the Trans-Siberian Railroad system [i.e., the Chinese Eastern Railway] which passes through Manchuria." And, since the Chinese already had troops near Harbin, and could send more, this was not an empty gesture.

A second move was based on the old adage of publicly commiting a suspect to a self-denying pledge as a way of preventing the crime. Wilson and Lansing had a perfect opportunity to do this: a Japanese spokesman had voluntarily offered such assurances. It is not so often realized, however, that France and the other allies were also concerned to check Japan. Perhaps the intensity of the French desire to act has obscured this point. While it is true that neither France nor England were as sensitive to Japanese operations in Manchuria, or in North China, as the United States was, it is *not* true that they were indifferent to the implications of an unrestrained Japanese move into the mainland — particularly in view of Tokyo's seizure of Shantung Province, and its Twenty One Demands of 1915. And, because it was a late-comer to the scramble for concessions in Asia, and because it was rather self-conscious about its lack of success prior to the war, Italy manifested an even stronger resistance to unilateral, unchecked Japanese intervention.

Lansing had clear evidence of this concern before Wilson acted between February 27 and March 1. The French were "very emphatic" and very explicit: "A full understanding and agreement would have to be had with Japan by all the other leading Allied powers, providing for the retirement of Japanese troops from Russian soil after the war, in addition to certain other guarantees." As if to make doubly sure that the meaning was understood, the French "evinced a keen curiosity as to the reason for the United States Government's opposing exclusive Japanese intervention."

France ideally preferred to bind Japan with a treaty, but Lansing demurred: that approach would involve the Senate, and the ensuing debate would cause jarring complications. A full, public discussion of policy toward Russia was not desirable from the point of view of the Wilson administration. That would open the way for Robins, Thompson, and other critics to force modifications in — or perhaps even a major change of — existing policy. The European powers acquiesced, and expressed themselves as being "quite satisfied with the way the matter is being handled by the President."

This support from England, Italy and France for the maneuver to control the Japanese encouraged Wilson and Lansing to feel, at least temporarily, and in conjunction with reports from Reinsch, Summers, and other American agents, that they could move in behind the Japanese and influence events in Russia along American lines through the use of economic power and diplomatic influence. Wilson's memorandum of the night of February 27 was a device to commit the Japanese to their own professions of moderation by announcing them publicly as the basis for American acquiescence in intervention. The United States, Wilson explained, "wishes to assure the Japanese Government that it has entire confidence that in putting an armed force into Siberia it is doing so as an ally of Russia, with no purpose but save Siberia from the invasion of the armies and intrigues of Germany with entire willingness to leave the determination of all questions that may affect the permanent fortunes of Siberia to the Council of Peace."

This sly but all-inclusive caveat was intended to trap the Japanese. On the one hand, they dared not reject such a pleasant essay in praise of their integrity. On the other hand, it would do them no good to ignore it because in that contingency the United States could use it as an aide memoire of an understanding based on earlier Japanese assurances. And, armed with the support of its European associates, America could feel confident of winning its point at the peace conference. In a real sense, Wilson was warning Japan to observe the conditions he specified or face united opposition.

Within 72 hours, however, Wilson withdrew even this support for Japanese intervention. The change, he told Polk, was "absolutely necessary." Several reasons account for the abrupt shift. The President was repeatedly and vigorously warned that the United States could not count on controlling Japan through the strategem of a self-denying pledge. These critics, such as Colonel House, argued that Wilson's approach risked creating an awful choice for the United States if the Japanese should decide to stay in Siberia, or turn their troops southward into China. If either of those conditions developed, the United States would have either to abandon the Open Door Policy or go to war against Japan. This analysis served to dramatize the second negative consideration, which was simply that Wilson was not ready to move immediately with a program of economic aid that would buttress American influence and also strengthen Russian and Chinese opposition to Japan.

In addition, the President also seems to have reconsidered the broad situation and, as a result, to have fallen back on the original strategy of December 1917, which was based on the axiom that direct intervention would provoke the Russians to support the Bolsheviks. Some Americans felt this would be particularly apt to occur if the Japanese went in alone; their reasoning being that racial antagonisms would be intensified by the memory of the Russian defeat in the Russo-Japanese War. And, finally, Wilson's central moral dilemma about intervention had been sharpened by reminders from men like Colonel House. They emphasized the loss of American influence if the principle of self-determination was so blatantly ignored.

All in all, the reversal of policy may well have been Wilson's finest moral hour. Torn by the conflict between his opposition to the Bolsheviks, which involved his entire political, economic, and social philosophy, and his deep involvement with the essential right of self-determination, the President chose to honor the moral axiom. Wilson's moral courage was no doubt reinforced by the fear that, given the existing circumstances, the Japanese outlook would triumph instead of his own. But that consideration should not be allowed to obscure either the intensity of Wilson's moral turmoil over intervention, or the central relationship between that agony and the change in policy. A man so essentially moralistic as Wilson could hardly be expected to view the Bolsheviks as anything but heretics, and to such men the heretic is even more dangerous than the non-believer. In this sense, at any rate, the surprise lies not so much in

Wilson's final intervention, but rather in the strength and persistence of his moral qualms about such action. The liberal conscience ultimately broke down, but its initial resistance was greater than sometimes seems to be the case long after the crisis.

While it did not cause Wilson's change of mind, the Italian opposition to unilateral Japanese action may well have encouraged the President as he reconsidered the issue. Clearly seeking to creep in under the umbrella of the Open Door Policy, Italy made "three conditions" for its support of any Japanese move. Tokyo's action "should be satisfactory" to the United States, the intervention "should be *not* by Japan alone," and "guarantees should be given by Japan that they do not intend to hold territory."

Wilson's circular note of March 5, announcing that he now opposed unilateral Japanese intervention provides what is almost a diagram of his thinking on the general subject. He remarked first on the "most careful and anxious consideration" that he had given "to the extreme danger of anarchy" in Siberia. This social and political situation was the root cause of the crisis, and intervention might in the end be necessary to control matters before they got completely out of hand. But he was "bound in frankness to say that wisdom of intervention seems . . . most questionable." Then, in what was at once a veiled expession of his fears about Japan and his commitment to the right of self-determination, he warned that all the assurances in the world would not prevent "what Germany is doing in the West."

In conclusion, Wilson revealed that he had fallen back on the strategic estimate evolved early in December 1917. Military intervention would generate "a hot resentment" in Russia, "and that whole action might play into the hands of the enemies of Russia, and particularly the enemies of the Russian revolution, for which the Government of the United States entertains the greatest sympathy in spite of all the unhappiness and misfortune which has for the time being sprung out of it."

And to Wilson, as to American leaders in general, the Bolsheviks were both the cause and the substance of that unhappiness and misfortune. In their minds, at any rate, the Bolsheviks were not considered part of the Russian Revolution for which the United States entertained "the greatest sympathy." As Assistant Secretary of State Long put it in a personal letter to Reinsch, American policy was concerned with supporting "the original revolution."

THE DECISION TO INTERVENE

Wilson did not abandon the idea of intervention on March 5; he merely refused to support one of many tactics of intervening. The President continued his search for some way to go into Siberia as the dominant power in an Allied force including Japan and then begin economic and political operations in support of the anti-Bolshevik movement. There is no evidence that the discussions to evolve an effective way to accomplish this objective had been significantly influenced by the occasional rumors about German military operations in Siberia. Lansing reviewed these stories in a memorandum to Wilson on March 19, and concluded that Admiral Knight's evaluation was valid.

Knight concluded that it was "impossible" for any significant part of the military stores in Vladivostok to be destroyed; that there was "absolutely no danger" they would reach the Germans; and that there was "no evidence" of any serious German influence in Siberia. He added that Lenin and Trotsky, and their Bolshevik followers in the Far East, were revolutionaries — not German agents. And he concluded with a strong recommendation that it was "of first importance" that Japan "should not be permitted to act alone."

Lansing did become somewhat concerned, between March 21 and 24, 1918, over a new flurry of reports that the Bolsheviks were converting some German and Austrian prisoners-of-war to their radical ideology, and then using them in military operations against the anti-Bolshevik forces in Siberia. If this turned out to be true, the Secretary anticipated that "we will have a new situation in Siberia which may cause a revision of our policy." His reference to a "new situation," makes it clear that neither the Bolshevik-as-German agent theory, nor the fear of a German campaign in Siberia, was a causative factor in the discussions of intervention that took place between November 7, 1917, and March 20, 1918. Lansing's approach to the new reports, furthermore, was wholly conditional. He was merely doing what any responsible official would have done: "we should consider the problem on the hypothesis that the reports are true and be prepared to act with promptness."

Wilson commended the Secretary for his foresight, but did not think the situation called for action. "I do not find in them," he replied, "sufficient cause for altering our position." The stories reappeared from time to time, but decisions were not made on the assumption that they were true. In April, for example, both Reinsch and the Czech leader Thomas Masaryk advised Wilson and Lansing that the tales were not worth serious attention, and most certainly were not a reliable basis for policy decisions. Reinsch's estimate was based on extensive first-hand information. He put "much work" into his efforts to find out what was going on in Siberia, and his chief agent in the field, Major Walter S. Drysdale (the American military attaché in Peking) was a man with "a great deal of good sense."

An early report to Reinsch, prepared by a Colonel Speshneff on March 9, told of finding the prisoners employed "as clerks, [and] some of them work as painters, carpenters, shoemakers, tailors, hairdressers, etc." Speshneff wanted American intervention "in the internal affairs directed against the Bolsheviki," but he did not base his plea on the danger from the prisoners-of-war. He was simply against the Bolsheviks. Drysdale's review on March 19 of the evidence he had collected during a field trip was unequivocal: "not a single armed prisoner was seen and there is little probability that any of the prisoners are armed." Three weeks later, on April 10, he reaffirmed that estimate. "Some very few of the prisoners" at Chita were being converted politically, and were "fighting as workmen, for the workmen's cause, against the Bourgeoisie."

As one Austrian explained to Drysdale, "they were helping their brother laborers in Russia against Semenoff and the Bourgeoisie." This situation might with some accuracy have been described under the heading of Austrians-as-Bolsheviks, but it was positive disproof of the argument that the Bolsheviks were German agents. And, as the men on the scene reported, there were no other armed prisoners. These on-the-spot dispatches, and Reinsch's summary of them for Washington, put an end even to Lansing's conditional and hypothetical worry about the prisoners-of-war.

On the other hand, the idea of supporting the Bolsheviks against Germany con-

tinued to show life. Robins sustained his campaign for that policy to the point of antagonizing consul Summers beyond his endurance. But, when Summers asked for a transfer, Lansing promptly and effectively exerted pressure on the Red Cross directors to recall Robins from Russia. That did not put an end to the advice to collaborate with the Bolsheviks, however, for American military representatives continued to recommend the same policy after Robins was ordered to return to the United States.

These men, who had agreed with Judson's estimate of the situation in November and December 1917, had no illusions about a political honeymoon with the Bolsheviks. They understood that Lenin and Trotsky were fighting the Germans to save the revolution — not as a disinterested favor to the Allies. Some of them also have sensed, as Robins did, that the Bolsheviks were becoming aware that they — or any Russian government, for that matter — needed allies against Japan and Germany. Even before World War I, Robins had concluded from a general analysis of the world political system that an American-Russian entente offered security for both countries.

The military representatives may not have gone that far in thinking, but they did argue that short-run collaboration was the most intelligent and practical course of action. Ambassador Francis allowed them to continue their discussions with Trotsky, and even to offer some technical assistance, even though he intended that any army organized by Trotsky would be "taken from Bolshevik control" and used against the revolutionaries. He thought any agreement with the Bolsheviks would help sustain them in power, and considered that "cost will be too dear."

Sometime in the second or third week

of April, at a stage when the German prisoner-of-war scare had been thoroughly discredited, President Wilson began an active search for some anti-Bolshevik group through which he could inject American power directly into the Russian situation. "I would very much value a memorandum," he advised Lansing on April 18, "containing *all* that we know about these several *nuclei* of self-governing authority . . . in Siberia. It would afford me a great deal of satisfaction to get behind the most nearly representative of them if it can indeed draw leadership and control to itself." Like the decision of December 10, 1917, to aid Kaledin in southern Russia, this letter makes it clear that American policy-makers were thinking of intervention as an anti-Bolshevik operation. The problem in the spring of 1918 was to find a winner; not only, of course, in order to defeat the Bolsheviks, but also to block the Japanese.

Further conversations between the two men seem almost certainly to have taken place during the next few days, even though no written record survives. This is strongly suggested, for example, by a dispatch Lansing sent to the American Ambassador in France on April 23. For, in briefing the Ambassador so that he would be able to discuss intervention with the French authorities, the Secretary clearly implied that such talks had occurred. Belgium and Italy, Lansing explained, had requested the United States to move a total of 450 officers and men, along with some armored cars, from Nagasaki and Vladivostok to the western front. *Acting on its own,* the American government had suggested in reply that it would be wise to leave the troops in the Far East.

That reply, Lansing explained, "was predicated upon the possibility of intervention in Siberia. It seemed inadvisable to bring away from there troops carrying flags of co-belligerents when it might be embarrassing to send back there other such troops." This action did not commit Wilson and Lansing to intervention, but it certainly indicates that they were discussing it seriously enough to keep non-Japanese troops in readiness. This conclusion is reinforced by Lansing's final cautionary word to the American Ambassador in France: "it is felt to be highly desirable that the matter should not be discussed with other persons."

Lansing and Wilson kept a sharp watch on the progress of the anti-Bolshevik leader Grigori Semenov during the ensuing month. Semenov was a Cossack who had served first as a Tsarist officer; then, after the March Revolution, he had gone to Siberia to raise a volunteer force of Mongols to battle the Germans. Caught in the east when the Bolsheviks took power, Semenov promptly began to fight them. He was vain, arrogant, and undemocratic, but his nerve and ruthlessness made him effective in the field — at least for a long enough time to attract the attention of American policy-makers. And, since neither Wilson nor Lansing favored negotiating any understanding with the Bolsheviks about intervention in Siberia, Semenov attracted their interest and concern.

The Secretary of State made it clear that he opposed any agreement with the Bolsheviks, even for the purpose of checking the Germans or the Japanese, because that "would array us against Semenov and the elements antagonistic to the Soviets." That should not be done. Wilson agreed, and on May 20 reiterated his instructions of April 18: "follow very attentively what Semenov is accomplishing and whether or not there is any legitimate way in which we can assist."

The President's clear and persistent concern to evolve some way of aiding the anti-Bolsheviks was reinforced during these weeks by an increasing campaign involving various anti-Bolshevik groups in the United States. They wanted to move in with economic aid, and then stay for a share in the post-Bolshevik economic pie. Wilson was interested in such plans, but his own thinking about intervention ran along the more narrow and specific line of aid to the anti-Bolshevik groups in their military operations. The door had to be opened, as it were, before the economic benefits — and influence — could flow through it. The President's approach of course involved economic assistance, but not in the precise form then being advocated by the various clusters of opinion in the United States. This difference between their outlooks became apparent in a second letter of May 20 from Wilson to Lansing.

A dispatch from Reinsch urging action prompted Wilson to ask the Secretary if the moment for intervention had arrived. "Situation in Siberia seems more favorable than ever," Reinsch judged on May 16, "for effective joint action of Allies and American initiative . . . Should America remain inactive longer friendly feeling is likely to fail." Lansing was definitely interested in Reinsch's argument, perhaps even partially persuaded, but not wholly convinced.

He was aware that Semenov's "policy is to keep the Siberian Railway open and overthrow the Bolsheviki," and that his successes offered "the prospect of forcing an amalgamation of all the different elements seeking reconstruction in Siberia." But the Secretary still worried about the danger of antagonizing the rank and file anti-Bolshevik Russians, even though support for Semenov could be combined with assistance to the Czecho-Slovak troops that were in Siberia. Lansing concluded, therefore, that the time was not yet "opportune" for direct intervention.

Wilson admitted the importance of not antagonizing the non-Bolshevik Russians, and of checking the Japanese, but those tactical difficulties did not lead him to abandon the search for a way to implement the strategy of anti-Bolshevism. He was prepared, as he told the British, to "go as far as intervention against the wishes of [the Russian] people knowing it was eventually for their good providing he thought the scheme had any practical chance of success." Joint intervention offered good possibilities of rallying the people against the Bolsheviks, but unilateral Japanese action would probably antagonize all the Russians "excepting for a small reactionary body who would join anybody to destroy the Bolsheviks."

Asked if this meant that the Allies should "do nothing at all," Wilson replied "No." "We must watch the situation carefully and sympathetically and be ready to move whenever the right time arrived." While waiting for an invitation to intervene from a successfully organized anti-Bolshevik group, Wilson wanted to prepare the way for effective operations by strengthening the economic situation in the non-Bolshevik areas of Siberia. Even as the President was thus reiterating his commitment to the fundamental strategy of anti-Bolshevik intervention, Lansing was modifying his tactical caution.

The Secretary received on May 26 a long letter from George Kennan, an old friend who was generally considered to be one of America's leading experts on Russian affairs. Kennan's advice and recommendations were militantly anti-Bolshevik. Lansing was impressed. "I have read the letter with especial interest because it comes from the highest authority in America on Russia." The Secretary naturally found it "gratifying that his own views were very similar" to those expressed by Kennan. The only significant disagreement concerned the "wisdom of intervention in Siberia."

Kennan was convinced that intervention was tactically workable as well as strategically desirable. Lansing wholly agreed on the strategy of anti-Bolshevism, but was "not so sure" that the tactic of direct intervention would prove successful. He explained, however, that the issue was receiving "very careful consideration" by the administration. And, because Kennan "had so clearly analyzed the state of affairs," Lansing promised to "lay it [the letter] before the President."

Lansing received more of the same kind of advice when he returned to the Department of State the next morning. A dispatch from Ambassador Page in London advised the Secretary that a League for the Regeneration of Russia in Union with Her Allies had been established in Rome, and was receiving support from Russians in England. It was militantly anti-Bolshevik, appealed directly to the United States for aid and suggested a "strong central government around which all sane elements would group themselves against Bolsheviks and Germans."

As he considered this development, the Secretary learned that the Allied ambassadors in Paris had agreed on the necessity and wisdom of intervention. They argued that it "must take place with or without the consent of the Bolshevik government," which in itself "has become far less important." Next, on May 30, Reinsch added his "urgent appeal" to act on the "extreme need for Allied action in Siberia." Russia, he explained, "is craving for order and will follow those who establish it. Only if established through Allied assistance will order be compatible with development of democracy."

All this was enough to prompt Lansing to warn Francis once again of the extreme care required in any ad hoc dealings with the Bolsheviks. "I am confident," the Secretary hopefully reminded the Ambassador, "you will appreciate the delicacy with which your actions . . . must be conducted." The Bolsheviks must not be allowed to receive or create any impression of American collaboration or assistance that would "alienate the sympathy and confidence of those liberal elements of Russian opinion which do not support Bolsheviki." As these instructions suggest, policy-makers in Washington were moving ever more rapidly toward overt intervention in support of their established anti-Bolshevism, and they wanted to rally all possible Russian support for the action.

On the next day, June 2, Lansing learned that a unit of Czecho-Slovak troops in Siberia had engaged the Bolsheviks. These men had fought with the Russians after deserting from the Austrian Army, but the Treaty of Brest-Litovsk left them without a war, and arrangements had been made by the French and the embryonic Czech government-in-exile, in negotiations with Lenin and Trotsky, for them to proceed via Siberia to the western front. Given the tensions in Russia, it would have taken a combination of great patience, extraordinary discipline, excellent communications, and unusual luck for such a contingent to avoid some clashes with the Bolshevik regional authorities. The odds against a peaceful remove to Vladivostok were simply too great, and a series of bitter outbreaks occurred along the Trans-Siberian Railway.

Lansing's first response in this situation was to assure Ambassador Page of the administration's sympathy and concern with the anti-Bolshevik League for the Regeneration of Russia. "Deeply interested in program for regeneration of Russia," he replied, "with which this Government, in the main, agrees." Then he alerted Francis to the increasing possibility of intervention through the subtle device of telling the Ambassador that the Department was "considering carefully" his own proposal of May 2 for such action. Assistant Secretary Long shortly thereafter reviewed for Lansing the advantages offered by intervention in liaison with the Czechs. They were "antagonistic to the Bolsheviks," and "available to be used as a military expedition to overcome Bolshevik influence, and under Allied guidance to restore order." As indicated by these and other dispatches of the period, American policy-makers straightforwardly discussed intervention as an anti-Bolshevik operation.

As the momentum for intervention increased among government policy-makers, Lansing became somewhat worried by a growing public discussion of the issue. The Secretary was afraid that the agitation would force the government to move before it was ready. Referring to the criticism of the government for the breakdown and failure of the aircraft construction program, Lansing warned against losing control of the intervention issue in a similar manner. "I see signs," he wrote Wilson on June 13, "in Congress and outside of a similar situation arising in connection with Russia." The Secretary's idea was to have Herbert Hoover take charge of an economic commission that would in turn provide an excellent public image of intervention. "Armed intervention to protect the humanitarian work done by the Commission," Lansing noted, "would be much preferable to armed intervention before this work had begun."

Wilson probably appreciated the political finesse inherent in Lansing's suggestion, but the President was strongly in-

clined to proceed first with armed intervention in support of the Czechs and other anti-Bolshevik forces. In that frame of mind, he responded favorably to Reinsch's analysis of June 13. Reinsch was very high on the Slavs: with "only slight countenance and support they could control all of Siberia against the Germans." The minister's reference to Germans did not mean that he had changed his mind about the nature of the Bolsheviks or about the danger of a German conquest of Siberia. He knew from Drysdale that the Czechs were anti-Bolshevik, and agreed with his subordinate that it was crucial to keep the Bolsheviks from mounting an effective counterattack.

The reference to Germany concerned his fear that an increasing number of prisoners-of-war might side with the Bolsheviks in view of the Czech attacks. He did not anticipate a German offensive in Siberia. Neither Wilson nor Lansing misread Reinsch's dispatch to mean that the nature of the danger had become German instead of Bolshevik. The President saw the Czechs as a strong, effective force which he could support against the Bolsheviks, and one which was also anti-Japanese and anti-German. That was precisely the kind of a nucleus he had been looking for since at least as early as the middle of April.

Wilson's central line of thought, and its anti-Bolshevik nature, was clearly revealed in his reaction to a favorable review and estimate of the All-Russian Union of Co-operative Societies. The leader of that organization, after expressing his opposition to the Bolsheviks, asked the United States to take the lead in intervention. The President's comment of June 19 on the report indicates not only his anti-Bolshevik objectives, but suggests very strongly that he had made his personal decision to intervene. The co-ops, he remarked, should be considered "instruments for what we are now planning to do in Siberia."

This interpretation is reinforced by another move Wilson made on the same day. He asked Secretary of War Baker to prepare a campaign plan for Siberia, using as a starting point a memorandum which proposed to undertake intervention by gathering and organizing support from the bourgeoisie in Siberia and the rest of Russia. The Army's reply was drafted by Chief of Staff General Peyton C. March. The war, he argued, would "be won or lost on the western front." Siberian intervention, "considered purely as a military proposition," was "neither practical nor practicable" — "a serious military mistake."

Wilson overruled this argument during a White House conference on July 6, 1918. He did so in full knowledge of the German assault on the Western Front. He also knew that the Czechs had overthrown the Bolsheviks in Vladivostok, and that they offered a general base of operations against the Bolsheviks throughout Siberia. Lansing had the same information. He noted on June 23 that the Czechs were "fighting the Red Guards along the Siberian line," and added on July 2 that they were fighting "to eject the local Soviets." As he commented in a private memo in July, the Secretary did "not think that we should consider the attitude of the Bolshevik Siberians."

The White House conference made it clear that intervention was *not* designed to establish an eastern front against the Germans. That was "physically impossible." Furthermore, the discussion of the basic "proposition and program" made no reference to aiding the Czechs against either the German or the Austrian prisoners-of-war. That phrasing appeared only as part of the "public announcement" to be made in conjunction with Japan, and in the section of the memorandum enumerating the conditions which Japan would have to meet.

Neither was there any mention of German or Austrian prisoners-of-war, or of Bolsheviks as German agents, in Wilson's aide memoire of July 17, 1918. Though the document has often been described as rambling, fuzzy, and even contradictory, the truth of the matter is that Wilson was both lucid and candid. He discounted intervention as a maneuver to restore the eastern front, "even supposing it to be efficacious in its immediate avowed object of delivering an attack upon Germany," as "merely a method of making use of Russia." That would not help the Russians escape "from their present distress." The Bolsheviks were responsible for that distress.

As far as Wilson was concerned, the purpose of intervention was "only to help the Czecho-Slovaks consolidate their forces and get into successful cooperation with their Slavic kinsmen and to steady any efforts at self-government or self-defense in which the Russians themselves may be willing to accept assistance." The full significance of the word *only,* and of the phrase *Slavic kinsmen,* should not be missed. The *only* was a throwaway word for the simple reason that the Czechs supplied all that was necessary from the American point-of-view. For that reason, the *only* was directed at Tokyo and designed to specify American opposition to Japanese aggrandizement. In a similar vein, the phrase *Slavic kinsmen* was designed to reassure the Russians that the Japanese would be kept under control.

Since Wilson and other top American leaders knew the Bolsheviks to be radical social revolutionaries, and had repeatedly stated their opposition to them on that ground, the meaning of Wilson's aide memoire should be clear. American intervention in Russia was a long-debated and long-delayed tactical move in support of the basic anti-Bolshevik strategy that had been established in December 1917. "I don't think you need fear of any consequences of our dealings with the Bolsheviki," he wrote Senator James Hamilton Lewis on July 24, 1918, "because we do not intend to deal with them."

Lansing added his explicit documentation a bit later. Absolutism and Bolshevism were the "two great evils at work in the world today," and the Secretary believed Bolshevism "the greater evil since it is destructive of law and order." It was, indeed, the "most hideous and monstrous thing that the human mind has ever conceived." That estimate led Lansing in 1918 to recommend a course of action that was to plague Western statesmen for at least two generations. "We must not go too far," he warned, "in making Germany and Austria impotent."

PRESIDENT WILSON'S LAST AGONY

President Wilson continued to aid anti-Bolshevik forces in Russia well into 1919. For that matter, the last American troops did not leave Siberia until April 1, 1920. During those years and months, Wilson avowed his concern not only with the radicals in Russia, but also with "the dangers of Bolshevism" in the United States. "It will be necessary to be very watchful and united in the presence of such danger," he warned on the morrow of Armistice Day, 1918.

As for the difficulties which prevented intervention from attaining its objectives, both the President and Secretary Lansing left terse but sufficient comment. Wilson's explanation to Winston Churchill during a discussion of the issue at the Paris Peace Conference contained all the essentials. "Conscripts could not be sent and

volunteers probably could not be obtained. He himself felt guilty in that the United States had in Russia insufficient forces, but it was not possible to increase them. It was certainly a cruel dilemma." Lansing made the same point to George Kennan in a "personal and secret" letter. "I wish you to know that it was not lack of sympathy which prevented the employment of a large active force in Siberia . . . We were bound hand and foot by the circumstances."

American intervention in Russia does not present the historian with an insuperable problem or an impenetrable mystery. It did not involve any dark conspiracy among American leaders. Considered as history, and leaving the question of its wisdom as policy for each reader to decide to his own satisfaction, the record indicates that the action was undertaken to provide direct and indirect aid to the anti-Bolshevik forces in Russia. It was thus anti-Bolshevik in origins and purpose. The men who made the decision viewed the Bolsheviks as dangerous radical social revolutionaries who threatened American interests and the existing social order throughout the world. They did not consider them to be German agents, nor did they interpret the Bolshevik Revolution as a coup engineered by the Imperial German Government.

Despite their concern to defeat Germany and to check Japan in the Far East, American leaders repeatedly refused to explore the possibility of attaining those objectives through collaboration with the Bolsheviks. *This was not a hypothetical alternative.* In spite of their theoretical doctrine, and the suspicion and hesitance it created in their minds, the Bolshevik leaders made persistent efforts to establish such co-operation. This flexibility created one of those turning points in history at which no one turned. The primary reason this opportunity was never exploited was because American leaders proved in action to be more doctrinaire and ideologically absolutist than the Bolsheviks. What might have been can never be known, but it is clear that American leaders proved less concerned with those possibilities than with the preservation of the status quo. As had so often been the case in the past, the United States defined Utopia as a linear projection of the present.

The only central question that remains unanswered about intervention concerns Wilson's personal authorization for the official publication of the infamous Sisson Documents, which purported to prove that the Bolsheviks were German agents. Neither the British Government nor the American State Department accepted the documents as proof of that allegation. Both therefore refused to publish the material. The President bears sole responsibility.

This becomes even more impressive when it is realized that *Edgar Sisson himself discounted the documents as proof that the Bolsheviks were German agents*. He said this explicitly on February 19, 1918, in a cable to George Creel, his superior in the Committee on Public Information. "These are wild internationalists," Sisson explained, "who not only in the beginning but until lately were willing to have German support for their own ends of Revolution. Germany thought she could direct the storm but the storm had no such intention."

One can only wonder, since no documentary evidence has ever been found, if Wilson knew of and read this dispatch which was transmitted through the State Department. It would certainly help to know; for, early in March, the President privately and personally ordered Sisson to proceed straight to Washington without any further discussion of the documents he had purchased in Russia. We do know that Lansing refused to accept and publish the material under the seal of the Department of State, and that Sisson was an angry man when he left his confrontation with the Secretary at the end of the first week in May. And we know that Lansing later called Sisson "a dangerous person" in a warning about dealing with him in connection with official business.

Finally, of course, we know that Sisson prevailed upon Wilson to publish the forgeries. He did so behind Lansing's back, and despite the Secretary's explicit opposition. It is possible, but unlikely, that Sisson simply persuaded the President that the documents were genuine. Wilson's own estimate of, and attitude toward, the Bolsheviks belies such an explanation. And while it is conceivable, it is highly improbable, that the decision hinged upon some personal matter between Wilson and Sisson.

Thus the evidence points toward the conclusion that Wilson underwrote the publication of the documents as a way of rationalizing his decision to intervene against the Bolsheviks despite his commitment to the principle of self-determination. The President had been intensely aware of that dilemma from the outset of the crisis, and it had caused him great torment and anguish. But he had ultimately intervened. Yet, knowing Wilson, it seems extremely unlikely that the overt act resolved the personal and ideological agony. And so, perhaps as a last effort to ease that terrible pressure, the President acquiesced in Sisson's insistent pleas. If such was the case, then it was an appropriate curtain for the tragedy of intervention.

The historian and the citizen can choose from among several arguments concerning the wisdom of intervention. He can agree with Winston Churchill that the revolutionary baby should have been strangled at birth. He can feel with Raymond Robins that the first opening to the left should have been explored; that such a course might have prevented, or at least significantly mitigated, subsequent suffering endured by the entire world. Or he can fatalistically conclude that it all would have turned out just the same no matter what had been done differently between November 1917 and April 1920.

Whatever the final evaluation, however, it does seem both more accurate and more helpful to begin the process of reflection on the consequences of intervention with the awareness that the action was anti-Bolshevik in origin and intent.

N. *Gordon Levin, Jr.:* AMERICAN INTERVENTION: ### AID TO LIBERAL RUSSIA

N. Gordon Levin, assistant professor of history and American studies at Amherst College, first presented the essay below at the Spring 1967 meeting of the Organization of American Historians in Chicago. An expanded version of this paper may be found in his book entitled Woodrow Wilson and World Politics.

THE WILSON Administration's decision to intervene in Siberia in the summer of 1918 was based primarily on the Wilsonian desire to use American influence in support of Russian liberal-nationalism against the interrelated threats posed both by German imperialism and by Russian Bolshevism to Russia's March Revolution. Indeed, despite steady Allied diplomatic pressure on behalf of Siberian intervention, the Wilsonian decision to intervene came only after a series of fortuitous events, involving an armed conflict between Czech troops and the Siberian Bolsheviks, made it appear that a cooperative American-Japanese action in Siberia might be successful in buttressing the forces of the March Revolution in the Russian East against their Bolshevik and/or German opponents. It is true, of course, that opposition to German imperialism was the most manifest

and explicit motive behind the Allied supported American-Japanese intervention in Siberia. Yet it is equally true that anti-Bolshevism was both implicit and latent in the Siberian intervention, a latent anti-Bolshevism which would ultimately be most fully expressed in America's protracted if unsuccessful postwar efforts to foster a non-Communist and liberal Siberia long after the defeat of German imperialism.

In the period between the March and November Revolutions in Russia, Washington sought, through the Root Commission and other means, to extend moral and material support to the war effort of Russia's liberal and anti-German Provisional Government. The destruction of Russian Tsarism by the March Revolution had made Russia, in Wilson's eyes, a fit partner in a liberal crusade against German imperialism. Moreover, the new liberal Russia and the Wilsonians were to work together to cleanse Allied war aims thereby making these aims more attractive to both German and Allied liberalism. In this fashion, the Allied war effort was to be purified and strengthened, but, at the same time, the war was to be shortened by an appeal to German liberalism over the heads of the German Government. The detailed analysis of Wilsonian policy and ideology during the war is another and complicated task, but for our purposes here it is important to note that in Russia the Wilsonian vision was quickly undermined by the destruction of liberal and social-democratic forces sympathetic to Wilson's values after the coming to power of Bolshevism in November of 1917.

The Bolsheviks, for their part, had no intention of keeping Russia in the war as a loyal member of the Entente, and Kerensky's Wilsonian-oriented foreign policy was totally rejected, therefore, along with the liberal and social-democratic domestic program of the Provisional Government. Bolshevik ideology made no real distinctions between the autocratic-capitalism of the Central Powers and the more liberal-capitalism of the Allies. Indeed, for the Bolsheviks all forms of capitalism were seen as equally imperialistic, and Lenin naturally favored universal socialist revolution to bring an immediate and lasting peace, an end to all forms of capitalism and imperialism, and a socialist commonwealth of nations.

In the face of this new and radical challenge to the Allied war effort and to his entire world view of liberal reformism, Wilson sought to turn the clock back in Russia to the period of April-November 1917 when the President felt that a liberal partnership had existed between America and the new Russia. In this sense, the Fourteen Points Address of January 8, 1918 was, in part, an appeal to the Russian people, and to the Bolsheviks as well, to recognize the special threat of German imperialism and to return Russia to a purified Entente alliance. As such, this speech represented the clearest expression of Colonel House's more moderate version of Wilsonian anti-Bolshevism, an approach which emphasized the hope of converting Lenin to Kerensky's domestic and foreign policy by means of Allied war aims purification. In the early months of Bolshevik power, the President would oscillate between this milder House-oriented form of anti-Bolshevism and the more hard-line anti-Communism of Lansing, who had no faith in the possibility of turning Lenin into Kerensky by war aims revision or any other means.

In point of fact, the ideological gulf between Bolshevism and Wilsonianism was not to be spanned by a liberalization of Allied war aims. It is true that some of the Bolshevik leaders, especially in the Bukharin faction, were ready to fight Germany in the event that no German revolution materialized and German policy at Brest-Litovsk remained excessively imperialistic. Indeed, Lenin himself, while counseling a compromise peace, was prepared to fight if Germany gave him no survival option. Such a Bolshevik choice to resist Germany in early 1918, however, even if it had involved military aid from the Allies, would not have meant a return by Bolshevism to the social-democratic Kerensky position of war for the Russian nation state as a member of a liberalized Allied coalition. That is to say, any defense of their revolution by the Bolsheviks against Germany would not have been oriented to social-democratic and conventional patriotic goals and means, but was projected in Bolshevik plans to be a revolutionary war dedicated to the defense of communism and to the spread of revolution. The Bolshevik leaders were ideologically incapable of rejoining the Allies, despite Wilson's efforts to cleanse Allied war aims. By the same token, however, the Wilson Administration, despite the hopes of such Left-liberal spokesmen as Raymond Robins, was not really prepared to help either the consolidation or the spread of Bolshevism, even against the Germans, until and unless Leninism became Kerenskyism. Thus, in Washington, whatever else it did, the Bolshevik ratification of the Brest-Litovsk Treaty largely removed the possibility of the Bolsheviks launching a revolutionary war, in defense of communism, against both Germany and Russia's social-democrats and liberals, an action which would have raised serious political and ideological dilemmas for the Administration. After Brest-Litovsk, then, it would be easier for Wilson to move toward a policy which combined opposition to both Lenin and the Kaiser in revolutionary Russia, especially since, in the President's mind, the true Russia always remained, despite temporary Bolshevik control, intrinsically liberal and anti-German. Somehow this true Russia had to be saved from both Bolshevism and German imperialism and brought back into the liberal international order. One of the means finally chosen by the Administration to help accomplish this goal was to be the intervention in Siberia.

During the spring and early summer of 1918, many factors, in addition to constant diplomatic pressure from the Allies, combined to move the Wilson Administration toward a policy of Siberian intervention. Underlying all these factors, however, was the desire of the President and his advisers to support those Russian elements, favorable to a pro-Allied order of liberal-nationalism, whom Wilsonians felt were menaced in differing, and yet paradoxically related ways, by both German imperialism and Bolshevism.

In one sense, this continuing Wilsonian desire to revive the values and institutions of the March Revolution was testimony to the successful efforts of the representatives of the deposed Provisional Government to foster, in a receptive official Washington, the conception that the struggle against German imperialism in Russia was inextricably bound up with the ongoing struggle of Russian liberal-nationalism against Bolshevism. During the period from March to July, 1918, repeated appeals reached Washington from various centers of Russian anti-Bolshevik activity inside and outside of Russia. These were essentially appeals for American and Allied support of anti-Bolshevik and anti-German Russian elements who were anxious to repudiate the Brest-Litovsk Treaty, to re-establish the socio-political order of the March Revolution, and to resume the war as an ally of the Entente. These same messages also often urged the Allies to sponsor a program of joint military and economic intervention in Siberia in which Japanese influence could be balanced by that of the United States. The significance of these appeals from the viewpoint of an analysis of Wilsonian policy formation becomes clearer when it is noted that earlier in 1918 the Administration had vetoed an Allied plan calling for unilateral Japanese action in Siberia. Washington had assumed at that time that such unilateral Japanese intervention would appear imperialistic and might possibly unify all Russians under the Bolsheviks in an alliance with Germany against Japan. However, the evidence from diplomatic dispatches between March and July, 1918, clearly suggested that so long as an intervention were a joint one, in which America had as much influence as Japan, it would have the support of the overwhelming majority of the anti-Bolshevik Russians.

Indeed, so great was the desire for some outside help against Bolshevism on the part of liberal-conservative Russian elements that some of these began even to consider the idea of turning to Germany as an ally against Lenin. In the late spring and early summer of 1918, a steady stream of information reached the State Department to the effect that influential middle and upper class political groups in Russia were looking increasingly to Germany for the restoration of social order. During the same period, members of the Administration at home and abroad often coupled advocacy of intervention in Siberia with warnings that many anti-Bolshevik Russians who had hitherto been anti-German would soon turn to Germany for aid against the Bolsheviks unless an American-Allied intervention could somehow provide them with a way to oppose effectively both Bolshevism and German imperialism. In June, 1918, Colonel House, who by then favored a policy of American economic intervention in Siberia, urged Henri Bergson to tell Wilson "that Russia could not compose herself without aid from either the Central Powers or the Entente, and if the Entente did not attempt it, Russia would turn to Germany."

Also aware of this last trend was William C. Bullitt, the one representative of Left-liberalism in the State Department. Bullitt wrote in late June to a supposedly sympathetic Colonel House asking:

What do you think of the argument which is being advanced by gentleman investors of all races at present, to wit, that the Russian aristocracy and the bourgeoisie is about to join hands with Germany against the Soviets, and that, *therefore,* we must join hands with the aristocracy and the bourgeoisie against the Soviets in order to get one jump ahead of the Germans? To me this is the supreme diplomatic non sequitur.

For Bullitt, this argument was a *non sequitur* primarily because, like many other Left-liberals and socialists in America and the Allied countries, he hoped for some sort of a Wilson-Lenin united front in a quasi-revolutionary war against both German imperialism and anti-Soviet Russians. Administration decision makers, however, to say nothing of their domestic critics on the Right, could be expected neither to permit Germany to restore social order in Russia nor to resist these German plans in the pro-Soviet manner desired by Bullitt and Raymond Robins.

In the first place, Wilsonians, despite their opposition to Bolshevism, rejected any concept of an anti-Bolshevik understanding with Germany during the war. To have permitted Germany to use her military and economic power as the rallying point for Russian liberals and conservatives would have meant a long step toward both the recognition of a German sphere of influence in Russia and the eventual signing of the type of compromise peace, advocated by Lord Lansdowne, giving Germany largely a free hand in the East in return for concessions to the Allies in the West. Yet, if Wilsonians rejected any wartime anti-Bolshevik *rapprochement* with Imperial Germany, they also rejected, with equal certainty, the opposite position of an anti-German alliance with an unmodified Leninist regime in Russia. Thus, while the notion of a Wilson-Lenin united front against German imperialism appealed to many on the American left in the spring and summer of 1918, the Administration was not prepared to ally with a purely Bolshevik regime against both Germany and many Russian anti-Bolshevik elements. All the more reason, then, for Washington to prevent Germany from becoming the recognized defender of all Russian anti-Bolshevik groups, for then the only way for the Allies to have resisted German power in Russia would have been through an overt alliance with Lenin. Moreover, it is also clear why the Wilson Administration had both an ideological and a strategic stake in keeping alive the alternative of backing Russian liberal-nationalism against both German imperialism and the Bolsheviks. In this connection, it should also be recalled that the diplomatic dispatches from Russia in the winter and spring of 1918 made clear that even if some Russian defenders of the values of the March Revolution might be willing to turn in desperation to Germany as a last resort against Lenin, most anti-Bolshevik Russian elements ultimately preferred Allied aid in defeating communism and in annulling the Treaty of Brest-Litovsk.

Indeed, in a variety of ways, Wilsonians came, in the 1917–1918 period, to see the obviously disparate forces of German imperialism and Russian Bolshevism as paradoxically united, objectively if not subjectively, in opposition to a liberal and pro-Allied Russian solution. On one level, many in the Administration suspected correctly that Germany had been willing to risk some financial support for revolutionary socialism in Russia in the hope that the Bolsheviks and other sincerely revolutionary groups would disrupt the anti-German order of the March Revolution and thereby destroy the Russian war effort. Yet, the ultimate concern in Washington during 1918 was related to the probability that Germany, after initially aiding the Bolshevik Revolution for expediential reasons, would reverse her

field and reappear as the savior of anti-Communist Russians and gain a sphere of influence in Russia under the banner of counter-revolution.

A State Department memorandum sent to Lansing's desk in mid-June of 1918 reasoned that a "timely intervention" directed against both unmodified Bolshevism and German imperialism would be the best method of preventing wavering liberal and conservative Russian elements from deserting the Allied cause and accepting the expansion of German influence in Russia as the price of Berlin's assistance against Lenin. The heart of the analysis in this memorandum develops a conception of Germany's dual strategy of first aiding Bolshevism to disrupt the pro-Allied Provisional Government, and then switching roles in Finland, the Baltic States, and the Ukraine to reappear as the counter-revolutionary defender of social stability in an effort to consolidate the predominant position of German economic and political power in the formerly Russian areas "liberated" by the Treaty of Brest-Litovsk. Even the fraudulent Sisson Papers, which sought to portray the Bolsheviks as mere German agents and traitors to socialism, could not ignore the fact that in the winter of 1918 the Germans were turning on the Bolsheviks and supporting conservative elements in Finland, the Baltic States, and the Ukraine.

Such assumptions made it easier for official Washington to conceive of actions taken against Bolshevism on behalf of liberal Russian elements as also constituting blows against growing German influence in Russia. Powerful political and ideological forces were making anti-Bolshevism a corollary to the Wilsonian war effort against Germany. On one level, it was necessary to oppose the Bolshevik movement because it sought to undercut the remaining power of pro-Allied Russian national-liberalism and thereby, consciously or unconsciously, to help realize the first phase of Germany's grand design for Russia. Then too, if Germany were in the process of deserting the Bolsheviks, all the more reason for Wilsonians to oppose Lenin lest the anti-Bolshevik Russians be won to Germany. Largely in response to such concerns, the cables reaching the State Department from American diplomatic personnel in Russia during the months immediately following the Brest-Litovsk settlement almost uniformly expressed opposition to Bolshevism and urged a policy of support for anti-Bolshevik and anti-German elements in Siberia.

It is true that the Wilson Administration continued, between March and June of 1918, to resist British and French pressure for military action in Siberia. This was both because Wilsonians doubted the military wisdom of certain more grandiose Allied hopes for reviving an Eastern front via Siberia, and because there was a lingering fear in Washington that the entrance of Japanese troops into Siberia might alienate otherwise pro-Allied Russians. Nevertheless, it is equally true that the appeals of American diplomatic personnel and of anti-Bolshevik Russians for some sort of intervention in Siberia were not totally lost on Wilson and Lansing in this period. After March, 1918, the evidence suggests an increasing desire on both their parts to find a moral way to satisfy Allied demands and come to the aid of non-Bolshevik and pro-Allied Russian liberals in the creation of a Siberia free both of socialist revolution and German penetration.

In April, 1918, Wilson informed Lansing of his interest in the several nuclei of self-governing authority which were springing up in Siberia, and the President added that it would give him "a great deal of satisfaction to get behind the most nearly representative of them if it can indeed draw leadership and control to itself." In May, Wilson continued to express an interest in Siberian anti-Bolshevism by asking Lansing to follow attentively what the Cossack leader Semenov was accomplishing to see if there were "any legitimate way in which we can assist." On May 30th, William Wiseman, a British intelligence officer, reported to London on a conversation with the President in which Wilson had said that he would favor military intervention in Russia if the Allies were invited "by any responsible and representative body." In a somewhat similar vein, Lansing cabled Thomas Nelson Page, the American Ambassador to Italy, on June 4th, expressing his essential agreement with the program of the League for Regeneration of Russia. The League's program had been sent to the Department by Page a week earlier, and it called for Allied support of a democratic Russian regime which would oppose both the Bolsheviks and the Germans. Then too, in the late spring of 1918, there was considerable support amongst Wilsonian decision makers for a non-military program of economic assistance designed to penetrate Siberia with American goods and liberal values in an effort to aid orderly Russian elements in curbing both German economic influence and the prevailing socio-economic upheaval. In this last connection, Wilson expressed special enthusiasm to Lansing on June 19th regarding the views of a clearly anti-Bolshevik member of the All-Russian Union of Cooperative Societies who had pleaded for Allied economic aid to the Cooperative Societies in their effort to bring social order to Russia's East and to make possible Siberian resistance to German penetration. The President felt that such cooperatives might "be of very great service as instruments for what we are now planning to do in Siberia."

In June of 1918, a division of Czech troops on its way to the Allied lines in France via the Trans-Siberian Railroad found itself in conflict with the recently established Bolshevik authorities in Siberia. In the course of this conflict, anti-Bolshevik elements rallied to the side of the Czechs throughout Siberia, and, by the end of June, they and the Czechs had succeeded in bringing most of Russia east of the Urals back under the control of non-Bolshevik and pro-Allied Russians. The Wilson Administration naturally showed immediate interest in the Czechs and their anti-Bolshevik Siberian allies as the potential nucleus for a pro-Allied and orderly Siberia free from German and/or communist influence. On June 13, 1918, Paul S. Reinsch, the American Minister in China, cabled to the Department his view of the opportunities opened up by the presence of the Czech troops in Siberia:

It is the general opinion of the Allied representatives here in which I concur that it would be a serious mistake to remove the Czecho-Slovak troops from Siberia. With only slight countenance and support they could control all of Siberia against the Germans. They are sympathetic to the Russian population, eager to be accessories to the Allied cause, the most serious menace to the extension of German influence in Russia. Their removal would greatly benefit Germany and further discourage Russia. If they were not in Siberia it would be worth while to bring them from a distance.

Wilson, obviously interested in Reinsch's dispatch, told Lansing that "there seems to me to emerge from the suggestion the shadow of a plan that might be worked, with Japanese and other assistance. These people are the cousins of the Russians." The concern expressed by Reinsch as to countering German influence in Siberia had particular reference to the threat

seemingly posed by hundreds of liberated German-Austrian prisoners of war who were fighting with the Siberian Bolsheviks against the Czechs and their anti-Bolshevik Russian allies. Indeed, ever since the signing of the Brest-Litovsk Treaty, the Administration and its representatives abroad had been fearful that large numbers of Bolshevik-armed German war prisoners would aid in the suppression of a pro-Allied and liberal Siberia and would also serve as the opening wedge for eventual German penetration of the Russian East. In connection with these Administration anxieties as to the roles of Germany, the armed prisoners, and the Bolsheviks in wartime Siberia, it is important to keep in mind that Lansing saw German policy in Russia as calculated to move from an early stage of cooperation with Bolshevism against pro-Allied liberal nationalism to a second stage of increased German influence in alliance with anti-Bolshevik groups. In this sense the German prisoners in Siberia appeared to Washington to be active in the first stage and to embody the potential threat of the second stage. Many of these issues were well expressed by Reinsch who cabled Lansing his views on the Bolshevik-prisoner threat in Siberia two weeks before his cable of endorsement of aid for the Czechs:

Reports received here from all sources indicate extreme need for Allied action in Siberia. German influence extending eastward while armed prisoners, though strategically unimportant, facilitate pro-German organization. West Siberia, source of supplies, is at stake. Positive action is required in order to prevent Russian moderate elements in despair accepting German influence. Bolsheviks waiting for social revolution in western Europe cannot resist nor effectually organize.

Against this background, it is not surprising that American representatives in

Russia saw in the Czech troops a possible way to save Siberia from both Lenin and the Kaiser. In the late spring and early summer of 1918, the diplomatic dispatches from Russia were almost uniformly enthusiastic in their portrayal of a Siberia in which Czech troops in league with pro-Allied and anti-Bolshevik Russian elements were successfully defeating a coalition of Siberian Bolsheviks and pro-Bolshevik armed German war prisoners.

Recently historians have partly obscured the complex nature of American intervention in Siberia by attempting to portray it as motivated almost exclusively by *either* an anti-German *or* an anti-Bolshevik intent. The confusion arises from a tendency to view these two motives somewhat as mutually exclusive when, in reality, they were fused in a Wilsonian desire to oppose both Bolshevism and German imperialism in Russia on behalf of a pro-Allied and liberal-nationalist Russia. Putting the matter another way, it could be argued that anti-Bolshevism was the natural corollary to any Wilsonian war effort in Russia as long as Leninist revolutionary socialism was ruled out on ideological grounds either as a weapon against German imperialism or as an acceptable social system for Russia. The Wilson Administration, for its part, was never prepared to accept complete Bolshevik rule in Russia in order to enlist Lenin against Germany. It is true that there was some vague sentiment within the Administration in favor of getting a Bolshevik invitation for Allied intervention in Russia, and it is also true that some efforts were made by the Department in May to stimulate Bolshevik opposition to Germany by curbing the overt efforts of American personnel in Siberia to aid the anti-Bolsheviks. Nevertheless, whatever attempts to arrange an unofficial anti-German *modus-vivendi* with Lenin did

originate in Washington in the winter and spring of 1918 were more than counterbalanced both by the moral unwillingness of Wilsonians to recognize the domestic authority of the Bolshevik regime and by the Administration's concern lest even a minor *rapprochement* with Lenin serve to push anti-Bolshevik Russians towards an alliance with the Germans. Of course, Lenin's own unwillingness to see the Entente as morally superior to the Central Powers also helped to make him objectively pro-German in the eyes of official Washington. In other words, Lenin was just as opposed to the idea of aiding the Entente or the pro-Allied sociopolitical forces in Russia, as the Wilsonians were opposed to the idea of solidifying Bolshevik control in Russia in the process of opposing German imperialism.

In any event, the Czech presence in Siberia offered an excellent opportunity for the Administration to ally with Siberian elements favorable to Russian liberal-nationalism against what appeared in Washington to be a concrete manifestation of German-Bolshevik cooperation. In a confidential memorandum written early in July, Lansing argued that America had a clear duty to aid the Czechs against both the Germans and the Bolsheviks in Siberia:

This responsibility is increased and made almost imperative because they [the Czechs] are being attacked by released Germans and Austrians. I do not think that we should consider the attitude of the Bolshevik Siberians who have furnished arms to the German and Austrian prisoners for the purpose of attacking the Czecho-Slovaks . . . As soon as the danger from German and Austrian aggression is over the military forces will be withdrawn unless Russia desires further cooperation on their part in resisting the Central Powers and their allies.

It must be emphasized that when Lansing

recommended American aid to the Czechs in Siberia he was fully aware that the Czechs and their anti-Bolshevik Russian allies were combatting the Siberian Bolsheviks as well as the German prisoners. In this connection, Lansing had written to Wilson on June 23rd that:

The situation of the Czecho-Slovak forces in western Siberia seems to me to create a new situation which should receive careful consideration . . . it appears that their efforts to reach Vladivostok being opposed by the Bolsheviks they are fighting the Red Guards along the Siberian line with more or less success. As these troops are most loyal to our cause and have been most unjustly treated by the various Soviets ought we not to consider whether something cannot be done to support them? . . . Is it not possible that in this body of capable and loyal troops may be found a nucleus for military occupation of the Siberian railway?

If this letter explicitly merged anti-Bolshevism and anti-Germanism, these motives were implicitly fused on July 8th when Lansing and the Japanese Ambassador Ishii "considered the possibility of a friendly attitude by the Russians toward the Czecho-Slovaks thus aided and also the possible consequence of their forming a nucleus about which the Russians might rally even to the extent of becoming again a military factor in the war." Such a program operationally meant hostility to the Bolsheviks who were fighting both the Czechs and the Siberian anti-Bolsheviks, and who were opposed to any plan of bringing Russia back into the war on the Allied side. Indeed, the late spring and early summer of 1918 was a period in which the Bolshevik regime, seeking desperately to survive between the rival power-blocs until a socialist revolution could sweep Europe, moved in the direction of a temporary and expediential *rapprochement* with German power in the face of mounting Allied pressures in the northern ports and Siberia.

On July 17, 1918 the State Department sent a detailed *Aide-Memoire* to all Allied ambassadors which told of America's decision to intervene in Siberia with Japan, and outlined the aims of such a military-economic program. America's purpose was to support the Czechs and loyal Russians in building a liberal Siberia free of German control, and not to use Russia as a new battleground for Allied armies:

Military action is admissable in Russia, as the Government of the United States sees the circumstances only to help the Czecho-Slovaks consolidate their forces and get into successful cooperation with their Slavic kinsmen and to steady any efforts at self-government or self-defense in which the Russians themselves may be willing to accept assistance. Whether from Vladivostok or from Murmansk and Archangel, the only legitimate object for which American or Allied troops can be employed, it submits, is to guard military stores which may subsequently be needed by Russian forces and to render such aid as may be acceptable to the Russians in the organization of their own self-defense.

When it is remembered that these words were written by men who knew that the Czechs had been joined by the anti-Bolshevik and pro-Allied Russian elements (i.e. "their Slavic kinsmen") in combat against Siberian Bolsheviks and the liberated German war prisoners, the fact that America's action was directed both at German influence and at Bolshevism in Siberia becomes even more manifest. In June of 1919 Wilson would send a message to the Senate on Siberian policy in which the choice of words would reveal perhaps more specifically what the *Aide-Memoire* of July, 1918, had meant by "efforts at self-government":

This measure was taken in conjunction with Japan and in concert of purpose with the other Allied Powers, first of all to save the Czecho-Slovak armies which were threatened with destruction by hostile armies apparently organized by, and often largely composed of, enemy prisoners of war. The second purpose in view was to steady any efforts of the Russians at self-defense, or the establishment of law and order in which they might be willing to accept assistance.

While it is possible to debate exactly what Wilson did mean by the "establishment of law and order" in Siberia, America's efforts to buttress a variety of anti-Bolshevik possibilities in Siberia during late 1918 and all of 1919 make it clear that the President did not mean a Bolshevik Siberia.

The heart of the matter is that since the Administration recognized the March Revolution as the only valid expression of the Russian revolutionary impulse, it was possible for Washington implicitly to oppose Bolshevism while explicitly denying any intent either to interfere in Russia's internal affairs or to further counter-revolution in Russia. To put the matter another way, the Wilsonian definition of counter-revolution in Russia was a desire to reinstate Tsarism but *not* a desire to replace the Bolshevik regime with liberal-nationalism. Wilsonians appeared to feel that they were not intervening in Russia's internal affairs so long as they were simply steadying the efforts of "Russians" (i.e. liberal Russians) to reestablish non-Bolshevik and anti-German democratic institutions in Siberia. That is to say, as long as in Wilsonian ideology the *real Russia* was implicitly defined as the Russia of the March Revolution, with the "objectively" pro-German Bolsheviks beyond the pale until they were willing to become patriotic social-democrats, the fiction that American policy in Siberia did not constitute an interference in Russian internal politics could be sincerely maintained in Washington.

In the Wilsonian mind, the United States was simply acting as the impartial and disinterested friend of the "Russians" who were utilizing the opportunity given them by the Czechs to reconstruct Siberian political life along the lines of pro-Allied liberal order. In this general vein, Lansing enthusiastically wrote to Wilson on September 9, 1918 that:

Our confidence in the Czech forces has been justified and the fact that now a Russian military force of equal strength has joined them combined with the gratifying reception given the Czechs by the civilian population of the localities occupied is strong evidence to prove that the Russians are entirely satisfied to cooperate with the Czechs in Russia and that assistance to the Czechs amounts to assistance to the Russians.

Considering all the evidence there can be little question that for Lansing the only "Russians" really worthy of the name were non-Bolshevik and pro-Allied.

Operationally, then, Wilsonian non-interference in the internal politics of Siberia really amounted to a tendency to see all non-Bolshevik and pro-Allied elements as an undifferentiated mass known as "Russia" and also to a refusal to interfere in the disputes among the rival claimants of anti-Bolshevik and anti-German authority. On August 2, 1918, Acting Secretary of State Polk cabled to Caldwell, the American Consul at Vladivostok, to say that "this Government sympathizes with the desire of patriotic groups in Siberia to secure the restoration of order and the welfare of the population but is not prepared to assist any one movement or group as distinct from others." This statement, with its emphasis on the "restoration of order," is a superb example of the Wilsonian tendency in practice to exclude the Bolsheviks from the field of Russian politics within which American neutrality was to be operative.

In other words, America was neutral when it came to choosing amongst conservative, centrist, and moderate socialist Siberian elements. The Administration was not neutral, however, as between the liberal order desired by most of these groups, and the alternative of total Bolshevik rule. Indeed, in the fall of 1918 there were many·efforts on the part of the State Department to make it clear that American reluctance to choose amongst the rival pro-Allied and anti-Bolshevik Siberian groups was in no sense to be interpreted as a lessening of the Administration's desire to see Bolshevism kept out of Siberia. In this connection, Lansing wrote to Boris Bakhmetev, the Provisional Government's Ambassador to Washington, outlining both the Administration's fundamental anti-Bolshevism and its neutrality only in relation to the various pro-Allied Russian claimants of anti-Bolshevik authority:

As you are aware, this Government is not, at the present time, prepared to recognize any new government in Russia, though we watch with interest and hope for the future the various efforts which are being made to restore law and order under a stable government. I note that the conference at Ufa includes the names of many distinguished Russians and shall be very glad to be kept advised· as to the progress of this movement. As you are aware, the purpose of the United States to assist Russia by any practical means which may be devised remains unchanged. The fact that this Government does not see its way clear at the present time to recognize political movements at Ufa and elsewhere must not be construed as a lack of sympathy with the efforts of the Russian people to erect a government which is able to protect individual rights and to perform its international obligations.

Moreover, documents concerning the Administration's plans for currency reform in Siberia also reveal that Washington

hoped a liberal-nationalist Siberia would eventually rejoin a non-Bolshevik and pro-Allied regime throughout Russia. During 1919, the anti-Bolshevik Siberian leader Admiral Kolchak would carry Allied and American hopes in this regard.

Finally, however, a complete understanding of the place of the Siberian intervention in the grand design of Wilsonian world policy is not possible without some consideration of the problem of Japan. Certain historians have put Japanese-American relations in the forefront of their discussions of the Siberian intervention, and have argued that the prime motivation for Wilson's decision to intervene was a desire to check Japanese imperialism and preserve the Open Door in the Russian East. Recently, however, other historians have emphasized, more correctly I believe, the interpretation that the Siberian intervention is best viewed in the context of a growing wartime cooperation between America and Japan against the threats of German imperialism and Bolshevism in Asia.[1] From the

[1] This position is well argued by Burton F. Beers in his *Vain Endeavor: Robert Lansing's Attempt to End the American-Japanese Rivalry* (Duke University Press, Durham, N. C., 1962), pp. 120–148, and *passim*. Beers points out that Lansing was an earlier and stronger advocate of a Japanese-American *rapprochement* than Wilson, but the combination of war and the Bolshevik Revolution brought the President to join Lansing in seeking a wartime *modus vivendi* with Japan in China and in Siberia. Indeed, at Paris, Wilson proved more willing even than Lansing to compromise with Japan on the Shantung issue in order to absorb the Japanese into a new American-inspired system of great power cooperation in Asia under the League of Nations. Both Wilson and Lansing continued throughout 1919, according to Beers, to seek an effective method of cooperation with Japan in the creation of a non-Bolshevik Siberia. The failure of this joint effort in Siberia, due to the obstruction of the Japanese military and due also to the political-military failures of the Kolchak regime, ought not to obscure the fact that Wilson and Lansing did work for American-Japanese cooperation in Siberia to the end of 1919.

Wilson administration's standpoint, the Siberian intervention was in essence an uneasy experiment in American-Japanese collaboration aimed at containing German imperialism, checking Bolshevism, and co-opting a hopefully moderate Japan into an orderly Wilsonian system of rational international-capitalist cooperation among the major powers interested in commercial expansion in the Far East. Thus, while it is true, on one level of analysis, that Washington hoped American participation with Japan in Siberian affairs would check potential Japanese imperialism in the area and protect the Open Door, it is more important to note in addition that larger Wilsonian policy aims involved a projected cooperation between America and Japan in the creation of a new anti-German and non-revolutionary liberal order for Asia.

A tendency toward finding a basis of understanding with Japan in Asia was operative in the State Department throughout the 1915–18 period. At the time of Japan's Twenty-One Demands on China in 1915, Lansing had unsuccessfully advocated a compromise whereby the Open Door for American commerce in China would have been preserved in return for what amounted to American acquiescence in Japanese expansion into Manchuria and Shantung. Lansing's orientation was not followed at this time, however, and it is true that during 1915 and 1916 President Wilson sought, largely in opposition to Japanese policy in the area, directly to promote the Open Door, to extend American economic expansion in China, and to defend the principle of the territorial integrity of China. It must be emphasized, nonetheless, that during these early years Lansing never lost his desire to come to a final agreement with Japan in Asia. This desire was naturally reinforced in 1917 when the United States and Japan found themselves allies against Germany. In this context, then, the Lansing-Ishii agreement of November, 1917 emerged as an effort, prompted in part by the war, finally to gain Japanese acceptance of the Open Door and the principle of Chinese territorial integrity in return for a vague American recognition of the "special interests" of Japan in Manchuria and northern China.

By way of a corollary to the Lansing-Ishii understanding, the Administration also moved in 1917 and 1918 toward participation in the Second Consortium, a program of financial cooperation among the major powers interested in the commercial penetration of China. It was hoped in Washington that the consortium approach would wean Japan away from a commitment to an imperialistic policy of spheres of influence and bring about Japan's absorption into an international-capitalist system of commercial freedom and order in China. In other words, the Administration sought to support moderate elements in Japan who were willing to seek expansion within an American-inspired framework of the Open Door and political-financial cooperation in the Far East. In a letter to Commerce Secretary Redfield, Lansing succinctly outlined the aims of America's consortium policy which sought to control Japan by co-opting her into a program of American-Japanese cooperation in Asia:

As to the suggestions in your letter and in that of Mr. Oudin that we have lost interest in the future of China or have handed her over to exploitation by Japan, permit me to say that such is far from the case. On the contrary, we maintain a very great interest, if possible, an increased interest in China, but, the circumstances in which the world now finds itself are such that it is not desirable for us to compete with Japan, other nations being eliminated from competition, and we are now, as far as possible, joining with Japan. This is done for the very practical reason that it is better to do so than to leave the field undisturbed for Japan.

This wartime policy of cooperation with Japan for purposes of control was further reinforced by Administration fears lest pro-German military elements in Japan gain the ascendancy and bring Japan into an imperialistic alliance with Germany.

The point of this discussion is not to argue either that the course of Japanese-American relations was free of suspicion and friction during the war, or that the road to the attempted Japanese-American cooperation in Siberia was a totally smooth one. We have seen already that the Administration refused to support unilateral Japanese action in Siberia during the winter of 1918. There was also a good deal of friction between Japan and the United States in the late spring and early summer of 1918 over the question of the type of contribution the Japanese were to make to the military phase of the joint Siberian intervention. Moreover, it should also be noted in this connection both that Lenin counted on rivalry between America and Japan in Asia to protect the Bolsheviks, and that there was considerable anxiety among some Administration advocates of a policy of intervention in support of anti-Bolshevik and pro-Allied Siberians lest German and/or Bolshevik propaganda drive an irreparable wedge between America and Japan. Nevertheless, these Bolshevik hopes and interventionist fears in regard to Japanese-American friction proved largely groundless in the short run, since the politics of war and revolution in

Russia which moved the Administration toward intervention in Siberia also reinforced Washington's wartime propensity for cooperation with Japan.

On March 5, 1918 the State Department sent a note to the Japanese Government detailing the reasons why, at that point, Washington felt unilateral Japanese intervention in Siberia to be ill advised:

> The Government of the United States has been giving the most careful and anxious consideration to the conditions now prevailing in Siberia and their possible remedy. It realizes the extreme danger of anarchy to which the Siberian provinces are exposed and the imminent risks also of German invasion and domination. It shares with the governments of the Entente the view that, if the intervention is deemed wise the Government of Japan is in the best situation to undertake it and could accomplish it most efficiently. It has moreover the utmost confidence in the Japanese Government and would be entirely willing . . . to entrust the enterprise to it. But it is bound in frankness to say that the wisdom of intervention seems to it most questionable.

It should be pointed out that while this note rejected immediate and unilateral Japanese action, its tone was nonetheless friendly and it joined the Japanese in recognizing that anarchy (a common euphemism either for Bolshevism or for conditions inspired by Bolshevism) and German imperialism were legitimate causes of concern in regard to Siberian politics. A few weeks later, in a private memorandum, Lansing reasoned that it would be a mistake to alienate Japan since any eventual military action in Siberia would depend for its success in part on enthusiastic Japanese participation. It will be remembered also that by the late spring of 1918 diplomatic dispatches had made it clear to the Wilson Administration that anti-Bolshevik and pro-Allied Russian elements would not object to Japanese intervention in Siberia so long as the United States participated as well. It was only natural, therefore, that Wilsonian plans to assist the Czechs and their Russian allies against anarchy and German imperialism should have provided for a cooperative role for Japan. In short, just as Washington sought to contain Japanese imperialism in China by absorbing Japan's expansive energies into an international financial consortium, so too Washington hoped to co-opt Japanese power into a Wilsonian program for the building of a liberal Siberia.

Indeed, in late 1918 and throughout 1919, Washington would continue its efforts in Siberia and China to bring Japan into an orderly and non-revolutionary Far Eastern system of liberal-capitalist harmony. Yet, in a larger sense, these efforts to arrange for Russian and Asian stability would form but one phase of the Wilsonian effort at the Paris Peace Conference to build a world free both of traditional imperialism and revolutionary socialism. Had the President been able to achieve these aims, and erect a rational and peaceful liberal-capitalist world order under a League of Nations, Wilson would not simply have succeeded in his implicit goal of refuting Lenin's vision of inevitable intra-capitalist conflict and revolutionary necessity. The President would also have achieved his central aim, at once both progressive and conservative, of establishing, on the grave of German imperialism, an American-inspired world system, beyond both atavistic imperialism and socialist revolution, a centrist liberal world order in which, for Wilson, America's moral and material preeminence would have been assured.

Suggestions for Additional Reading

There is no full-length exhaustive study of the United States and the Russian Civil War. There are, however, a number of volumes which treat the subject within the context of Russian-American relations or American-Far Eastern relations in general. George F. Kennan, *Russia and the West under Lenin and Stalin* (Boston, 1961), is a provocatively written analysis of relations between Russia and the West, especially the United States, since the 1917 Revolution, which places rather heavy emphasis on the period from 1917 through 1921. Kennan is especially critical of Western statesmen for policies adopted toward the Soviet regime in these first critical years. Denna F. Fleming, *The Cold War and Its Origins, 1917–1960* (2 vols.; New York, 1961), covers the period from 1917 to 1920 in Volume I. He blames the West for the hostility between the East and the West. Two other studies highly critical of American policies, including non-recognition, are Frederick L. Schuman, *American Policy Toward Russia since 1917* (New York, 1928), and William A. Williams, *American-Russian Relations, 1781–1947* (New York, 1952). The latter sees American policies in the early period as largely inspired by American "capitalists." Pauline F. Tompkins, *American-Russian Relations in the Far East* (New York, 1949), sees American intervention in the Russian Far East determined largely by the American necessity to stop the Japanese drive for empire and defend Russian sovereignty in the Far East.

Of the specialized studies dealing with Soviet-American relations during this period certainly one of the most authoritative and well-written accounts is George F. Kennan, *Soviet-American Relations,* *1917–1920* (2 vols.; Princeton, 1956). Volume I, *Russia Leaves the War,* covers the period November 1917 to March 1918. Volume II, *The Decision to Intervene,* continues the story down to the desions which resulted in the sending of American forces to north Russia and Siberia. Christopher Lasch, *The American Liberals and the Russian Revolution* (New York and London, 1962), examines the attitudes of one group toward the cataclysmic events in Russia. More general is Leonid I. Strakhovsky, *American Opinion About Russia, 1917–1920* (Toronto, 1961). It is especially useful for its lengthy excerpts from the press illustrating contemporary confusion and misconceptions about Russian events. For Allied policy toward Bolshevism at the Paris Peace Conference, see John M. Thompson, *Russia, Bolshevism and the Versailles Peace* (Princeton, 1966).

On the North Russian expedition E. M. Halliday, *The Ignorant Armies* (New York, 1960), recounts in popular style the experiences and adventures of the 339th United States infantry regiment in North Russia. The author is critical of intervention in general and American participation particularly. The Russian emigré historian, Leonid I. Strakhovsky, who participated in some of the events recounted, has written two studies of the North Russian intervention, *The Origins of American Intervention in North Russia, 1918* (Princeton, 1937) and *Intervention at Archangel: The Story of Allied Intervention and Russian Counter-Revolution in North Russia, 1918–1920* (Princeton, 1944).

On American intervention in Siberia, the only full-length study of the American decision to intervene and its consequences is Betty Miller Unterberger, *America's Siberian Expedition, 1918–1920: A Study of National Policy* (Durham, 1956). The student desiring to know the effects of intervention on the Civil War in Siberia is directed to John A. White, *The Siberian Intervention* (Princeton, 1950), a scholarly account based on a broad range of published materials in several languages. An excellent account of British policy toward Russia is Richard H. Ullman, *Anglo-Soviet Relations, 1917–1921*, Volume I: *Intervention and the War* (Princeton, 1961). The standard work on the origins of the Japanese decision to intervene, based primarily on Japanese sources, is James W. Morley, *The Japanese Thrust into Siberia, 1918* (New York, 1957). For an analysis of gross Soviet misrepresentations of American motives and activities in the Russian intervention see George F. Kennan, "Soviet Historiography and America's Role in the Intervention," *American Historical Review*, LXV (1960), 302–322.

There are a number of colorful personal accounts, both official and unofficial, by individuals who were in Russia during this eventful period. Carl W. Ackerman, *Trailing the Bolsheviki: Twelve Thousand Miles with the Allies in Siberia* (New York, 1919), is a journalistic account of Siberian conditions with considerable emphasis on the actions of United States forces. The author was a special correspondent for the *New York Times*. Ralph Albertson, *Fighting Without a War: An Account of Military Intervention in North Russia* (New York, 1920), is a personal account by a former member of the YMCA who served in North Russia in 1918–1919. Arthur Bullard, one of the most intelligent and best informed of America's official observers, has written a thoughtful discussion of some of the most important problems of the revolu-

tionary period in the *Russian Pendulum: Autocracy-Democracy-Bolshevism* (New York, 1919). The testimony of Mr. William C. Bullitt concerning his mission to Russia in February-March 1919 appears in his *The Bullitt Mission to Russia: Testimony before the Committee on Foreign Relations* (New York, 1919). Exceedingly interesting, although not always authoritative, are the memoirs of the American Ambassador to Russia, David R. Francis, *Russia from the American Embassy, April, 1916–November, 1918* (New York, 1921). William S. Graves, *America's Siberian Adventure, 1918–1920* (New York, 1931), is a valuable account by the commander of the American expeditionary force, who was highly critical of the entire enterprise. William Hard, *Raymond Robins' Own Story* (New York, 1920), attempts to summarize what Robins had to say on his return from Russia in 1918. It is useful primarily as an estimate of Robins' image of himself and his work. For the role of Edward M. House, Wilson's intimate adviser, on Russian decisions see Volume III of Charles Seymour, ed., *The Intimate Papers of Colonel House* (4 vols.; Boston, 1926–1928). An interesting, well-written first-hand account by an American officer, although violently anti-Japanese, is Sylvian G. Kindall, *American Soldiers in Siberia* (New York, 1945). An invaluable source for the period, although not representing the American point of view, is the superbly written account by Robert H. Bruce Lockhart, *British Agent* (New York, 1932), of his experiences unofficially in contact with the Bolshevik regime, January to September 1918. Another interesting, well-written memoir by the head of the office of the Committee on Public Information in Petrograd (November 1917–February 1918) who was responsible for discovering and bringing to Washington the so-called Sisson Document, purporting to prove that Lenin was a German agent, is Edgar G. Sisson, *One Hundred Red Days: A Personal Chronicle of the Bolshevik Revolution* (New Haven, 1932).

The discriminating student who wishes to weigh the evidence for himself should be directed to the official documents themselves. The most valuable of these are: United States Department of State, *Papers Relating to the Foreign Relations of the United States, 1918, Russia* (3 vols.; Washington, 1931–1932). Volume I covers political affairs and diplomatic relations. Volume II is devoted to papers dealing with the anti-Bolshevik movements in Siberia and Manchuria, Murmansk, Archangel, and elsewhere, and Allied reaction to them. Volume III deals chiefly with loans to the provisional government, assistance to railway transportation and Soviet repudiation of the loans. United States, Department of State, *Foreign Relations of the United States, 1919, Russia* (Washington, 1937), covers intervention in 1919. It is vital although not as well organized as the 1918 volumes on Russia. In the same series *Foreign Relations of the United States, The Lansing Papers, 1914–1920* (2 vols., Washington, 1940), Volume II contains selected documents from the Secretary's correspondence on Russia and Siberia which are very helpful.

DATE DUE

GAYLORD   PRINTED IN U.S.A.